# The Famous Oz Books

Since 1900, when L. Frank Baum introduced to the children of America THE WONDERFUL WIZARD OF OZ and all the other exciting characters who inhabit the land of Oz, these delightful fairy tales have stimulated the imagination of millions of young readers.

These are stories which are genuine fantasy — creative, funny, tender, exciting and surprising. Filled with the rarest and most absurd creatures, each of the 14 volumes which now comprise the series, has been eagerly sought out by generation after generation until today they are known to all except the very young or those who were never young at all.

When, in a recent survey, The New York Times polled a group of teen agers on the books they liked best when they were young, the Oz books topped the list.

# THE FAMOUS OZ BOOKS

By L. Frank Baum:

THE WIZARD OF OZ
THE LAND OF OZ
OZMA OF OZ
DOROTHY AND THE WIZARD IN OZ
THE ROAD TO OZ
THE EMERALD CITY OF OZ
THE PATCHWORK GIRL OF OZ
TIK-TOK OF OZ
THE SCARECROW OF OZ
RINKITINK IN OZ
THE LOST PRINCESS OF OZ
THE TIN WOODMAN OF OZ
THE MAGIC OF OZ
GLINDA OF OZ

# THE SCARECROW of OZ

## Dedicated to

"The Uplifters" of Los Angeles, California, in grateful appreciation of the pleasure I have derived from association with them, and in recognition of their sincere endeavor to uplift humanity through kindness, consideration and good-fellowship. They are big men—all of them—and all with the generous hearts of little children.

L. Frank Baum

# THE
# SCARECROW OF OZ

BY

## L. FRANK BAUM

AUTHOR OF

THE ROAD TO OZ, DOROTHY AND THE WIZARD IN OZ, THE
EMERALD CITY OF OZ, THE LAND OF OZ, OZMA
OF OZ, THE PATCHWORK GIRL OF OZ,
TIK-TOK OF OZ

ILLUSTRATED BY

## JOHN R. NEILL

## Henry Regnery Company
## Chicago

Published by Henry Regnery Company
180 North Michigan Avenue, Chicago, Illinois 60601
Manufactured in the United States of America
Library of Congress Catalog Card Number: 76-014132
International Standard Book Number: 0-8092-7975-4

## 'TWIXT YOU AND ME

The Army of Children which besieged the Postoffice, conquered the Postmen and delivered to me its imperious Commands, insisted that Trot and Cap'n Bill be admitted to the Land of Oz, where Trot could enjoy the society of Dorothy, Betsy Bobbin and Ozma, while the one-legged sailor-man might become a comrade of the Tin Woodman, the Shaggy Man, Tik-Tok and all the other quaint people who inhabit this wonderful fairyland.

It was no easy task to obey this order and land Trot and Cap'n Bill safely in Oz, as you will discover by reading this book. Indeed, it required the best efforts of our dear old friend, the Scarecrow, to save them from a dreadful fate on the journey; but the story leaves them happily located in Ozma's splendid palace and Dorothy has promised me that Button-Bright and the three girls are sure to encounter, in the near future, some marvelous adventures in the Land of Oz, which I hope to be permitted to relate to you in the next Oz Book.

Meantime, I am deeply grateful to my little readers for their continued enthusiasm over the Oz stories, as evinced in the many letters they send me, all of which are lovingly cherished. It takes more and more Oz Books every year to satisfy the demands of old and new readers, and there have been formed many "Oz Reading Societies," where the Oz Books owned by different members are read aloud. All this is very gratifying to me and encourages me to write more Oz stories. When the children have had enough of them, I hope they will let me know, and then I'll try to write something different.

L. FRANK BAUM
"Royal Historian of Oz."

"OZCOT"
at HOLLYWOOD
in CALIFORNIA,
1915.

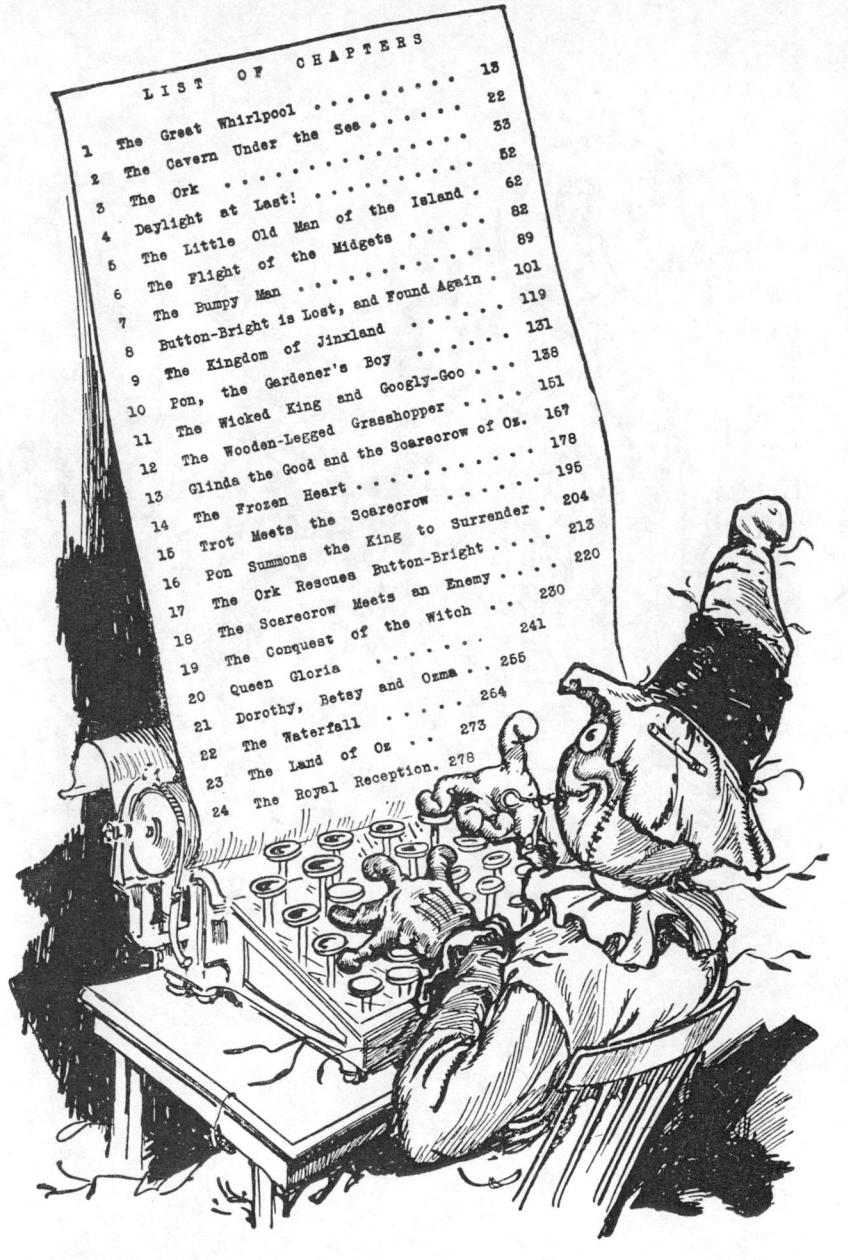

## CHAPTER 1

# The Great Whirlpool

"Seems to me," said Cap'n Bill, as he sat beside Trot under the big acacia tree, looking out over the blue ocean, "seems to me, Trot, as how the more we know, the more we find we don't know."

"I can't quite make that out, Cap'n Bill," answered the little girl in a serious voice, after a moment's thought, during which her eyes followed those of the old sailor-man across the glassy surface of the sea. "Seems to me that all we learn is jus' so much gained."

"I know; it looks that way at first sight," said the sailor, nodding his head; "but those as knows the least

**13**

have a habit of thinkin' they know all there is to know, while them as knows the most admits what a turr'ble big world this is. It's the knowing ones that realize one lifetime ain't long enough to git more'n a few dips o' the oars of knowledge."

Trot didn't answer. She was a very little girl, with big, solemn eyes and an earnest, simple manner. Cap'n Bill had been her faithful companion for years and had taught her almost everything she knew.

He was a wonderful man, this Cap'n Bill. Not so very old, although his hair was grizzled — what there was of it. Most of his head was bald as an egg and as shiny as oilcloth, and this made his big ears stick out in a funny way. His eyes had a gentle look and were pale blue in color, and his round face was rugged and bronzed. Cap'n Bill's left leg was missing, from the knee down, and that was why the sailor no longer sailed the seas. The wooden leg he wore was good enough to stump around with on land, or even to take Trot out for a row or a sail on the ocean, but when it came to "runnin' up aloft" or performing active duties on shipboard, the old sailor was not equal to the task. The loss of his leg had ruined his career and the old sailor found comfort in devoting himself to the education and companionship of the little girl.

# Chapter One

The accident to Cap'n Bill's leg had happened at about the time Trot was born, and ever since that he had lived with Trot's mother as "a star boarder," having enough money saved up to pay for his weekly "keep." He loved the baby and often held her on his lap; her first ride was on Cap'n Bill's shoulders, for she had no baby-carriage; and when she began to toddle around, the child and the sailor became close comrades and enjoyed many strange adventures together. It is said the fairies had been present at Trot's birth and had marked her forehead with their invisible mystic signs, so that she was able to see and do many wonderful things.

The acacia tree was on top of a high bluff, but a path ran down the bank in a zigzag way to the water's edge, where Cap'n Bill's boat was moored to a rock by means of a stout cable. It had been a hot, sultry afternoon, with scarcely a breath of air stirring, so Cap'n Bill and Trot had been quietly sitting beneath the shade of the tree, waiting for the sun to get low enough for them to take a row.

They had decided to visit one of the great caves which the waves had washed out of the rocky coast during many years of steady effort. The caves were a source of continual delight to both the girl and the sailor, who loved to explore their awesome depths.

"I b'lieve, Cap'n," remarked Trot, at last, "that it's time for us to start."

The old man cast a shrewd glance at the sky, the sea and the motionless boat. Then he shook his head.

"Mebbe it's time, Trot," he answered, "but I don't jes' like the looks o' things this afternoon."

"What's wrong?" she asked wonderingly.

"Can't say as to that. Things is too quiet to suit me, that's all. No breeze, not a ripple a-top the water, nary a gull a-flyin' anywhere, an' the end o' the hottest day o' the year. I ain't no weather-prophet, Trot, but any sailor would know the signs is ominous."

"There's nothing wrong that I can see," said Trot. "If there was a cloud in the sky even as big as my thumb, we might worry about it; but — look, Cap'n! — the sky is as clear as can be."

He looked again and nodded.

"P'r'aps we can make the cave, all right," he agreed, not wishing to disappoint her. "It's only a little way out, an' we'll be on the watch; so come along, Trot."

Together they descended the winding path to the beach. It was no trouble for the girl to keep her footing on the steep way, but Cap'n Bill, because of his wooden leg, had to hold on to rocks and roots now and then to save himself from tumbling. On a level path he was as spry as anyone, but to climb up hill or down required some care.

They reached the boat safely and while Trot was untying the rope Cap'n Bill reached into a crevice of the rock and drew out several tallow candles and a box of wax matches, which he thrust into the capacious pockets of his " sou'wester." This sou'-wester was a short coat of oilskin which the old sailor wore on all occasions — when he wore a coat at all — and the pockets always contained a variety of objects, useful and ornamental, which made even Trot wonder where they all came from and why Cap'n Bill should treasure them. The jackknives — a big one and a little one — the bits of cord, the fishhooks, the nails: these were handy to have on certain occasions. But bits of shell, and tin boxes with unknown contents, buttons, pincers, bottles of curious stones and the like, seemed quite unnecessary to carry around. That was Cap'n Bill's business, however, and now that he added the candles and the matches to his collection Trot made no comment, for she knew these last were to light their way through the caves.

The sailor always rowed the boat, for he handled

the oars with strength and skill. Trot sat in the stern and steered. The place where they embarked was a little bight or circular bay, and the boat cut across a much larger bay toward a distant headland where the caves were located, right at the water's edge. They were nearly a mile from shore and about halfway across the bay when Trot suddenly sat up straight and exclaimed: "What's that, Cap'n?"

He stopped rowing and turned half around to look.

"That, Trot," he slowly replied, "looks to me mighty like a whirlpool."

"What makes it, Cap'n?"

"A whirl in the air makes the whirl in the water. I was afraid as we'd meet with trouble, Trot. Things didn't look right. The air was too still."

"It's coming closer," said the girl.

The old man grabbed the oars and began rowing with all his strength.

" 'Tain't comin' closer to us, Trot," he gasped; " it's we that are comin' closer to the whirlpool. The thing is drawin' us to it like a magnet! "

Trot's sun-bronzed face was a little paler as she grasped the tiller firmly and tried to steer the boat away; but she said not a word to indicate fear.

The swirl of the water as they came nearer made a roaring sound that was fearful to listen to. So fierce and powerful was the whirlpool that it drew the surface of the sea into the form of a great basin, slanting downward toward the center, where a big hole had been made in the ocean — a hole with walls of water that were kept in place by the rapid whirling of the air.

The boat in which Trot and Cap'n Bill were riding was just on the outer edge of this saucer-like slant, and the old sailor knew very well that unless he could quickly force the little craft away from the rushing current they would soon be drawn into the great black hole that yawned in the middle. So he exerted all his might and pulled as he had never pulled before. He pulled so hard that the left oar snapped in two and sent Cap'n Bill sprawling upon the bottom of the boat.

He scrambled up quickly enough and glanced over

the side. Then he looked at Trot, who sat quite still, with a serious, far-away look in her sweet eyes. The boat was now speeding swiftly of its own accord, following the line of the circular basin round and round and gradually drawing nearer to the great hole in the center. Any further effort to escape the whirlpool was useless, and realizing this fact Cap'n Bill turned toward Trot and put an arm around her, as if to shield her from the awful fate before them. He did not try to speak, because the roar of the waters would have drowned the sound of his voice.

These two faithful comrades had faced dangers before, but nothing to equal that which now faced them. Yet Cap'n Bill, noting the look in Trot's eyes and remembering how often she had been protected by unseen powers, did not quite give way to despair.

The great hole in the dark water — now growing nearer and nearer — looked very terrifying; but they were both brave enough to face it and await the result of the adventure.

## CHAPTER 2

# The Cavern Under the Sea

The circles were so much smaller at the bottom of the basin, and the boat moved so much more swiftly, that Trot was beginning to get dizzy with the motion, when suddenly the boat made a leap and dived headlong into the murky depths of the hole. Whirling like tops, but still clinging together, the sailor and the girl were separated from their boat and plunged down — down — down — into the farthermost recesses of the great ocean.

At first their fall was swift as an arrow, but presently they seemed to be going more moderately and Trot was almost sure that unseen arms were about her, supporting her and protecting her. She could see nothing, because the water filled her eyes and blurred her vision, but she clung fast to Cap'n Bill's sou'-wester, while other arms clung fast to her, and so they gradually sank down and down until a full stop was made, when they began to ascend again.

But it seemed to Trot that they were not rising straight to the surface from where they had come. The water was no longer whirling them and they seemed to be drawn in a slanting direction through still, cool ocean depths. And then — in much quicker time than I have told it — up they popped to the surface and were cast at full length upon a sandy beach, where they lay choking and gasping for breath and wondering what had happened to them.

Trot was the first to recover. Disengaging herself from Cap'n Bill's wet embrace and sitting up, she rubbed the water from her eyes and then looked around her. A soft, bluish-green glow lighted the place, which seemed to be a sort of cavern, for above and on either side of her were rugged rocks. They had been cast upon a beach of clear sand, which slanted upward from the pool of water at their feet — a pool which doubtless led into the big ocean that fed it. Above the reach of the waves of the pool were more rocks, and still more and more, into the dim windings and recesses of which the glowing light from the water did not penetrate.

The place looked grim and lonely, but Trot was thankful that she was still alive and had suffered no severe injury during her trying adventure under water. At her side Cap'n Bill was sputtering and coughing, trying to get rid of the water he had swallowed. Both of them were soaked through, yet the cavern was warm and comfortable and a wetting did not dismay the little girl in the least.

She crawled up the slant of sand and gathered in her hand a bunch of dried seaweed, with which she mopped the face of Cap'n Bill and cleared the water from his eyes and ears. Presently the old man sat up and stared at her intently. Then he nodded his bald head three times and said in a gurgling voice:

"Mighty good, Trot; mighty good! We didn't reach Davy Jones's locker that time, did we? Though why we didn't, an' why we're here, is more'n I kin make out."

"Take it easy, Cap'n," she replied. "We're safe enough, I guess, at least for the time being."

He squeezed the water out of the bottoms of his loose trousers and felt of his wooden leg and arms and head, and finding he had brought all of his person with him he gathered courage to examine closely their surroundings.

"Where d'ye think we are, Trot?" he presently asked.

"Can't say, Cap'n. P'r'aps in one of our caves."

He shook his head. "No," said he, "I don't think that, at all. The distance we came up didn't seem half as far as the distance we went down; an' you'll notice there ain't any outside entrance to this cavern whatever. It's a reg'lar dome over this pool o' water, and unless there's some passage at the back, up yonder, we're fast pris'ners."

Trot looked thoughtfully over her shoulder.

"When we're rested," she said, "we will crawl up there and see if there's a way to get out."

Cap'n Bill reached in the pocket of his oilskin coat and took out his pipe. It was still dry, for he kept it in an oilskin pouch with his tobacco. His matches were in a tight tin box, so in a few moments the old sailor was smoking contentedly. Trot knew it helped him to think when he was in any difficulty. Also, the pipe did much to restore the old sailor's composure, after his long ducking and his terrible fright — a fright that was more on Trot's account than his own.

The sand was dry where they sat, and soaked up the water that dripped from their clothing. When Trot had squeezed the wet out of her hair she began to feel much like her old self again. By and by they got upon their feet and crept up the incline to the scattered boulders above. Some of these were of huge size, but by passing between some and around others, they were able to reach the extreme rear of the cavern.

"Yes," said Trot, with interest, "here's a round hole."

"And it's black as night inside it," remarked Cap'n Bill.

"Just the same," answered the girl, "we ought to explore it, and see where it goes, 'cause it's the only poss'ble way we can get out of this place."

Cap'n Bill eyed the hole doubtfully.

"It may be a way out o' here, Trot," he said, "but it may be a way into a far worse place than this. I'm not sure but our best plan is to stay right here."

Trot wasn't sure, either, when she thought of it in that light. After awhile she made her way back to the sands again, and Cap'n Bill followed her. As they sat down, the child looked thoughtfully at the sailor's bulging pockets.

Trot

"How much food have we got, Cap'n?" she asked.

"Half a dozen ship's biscuits an' a hunk o' cheese," he replied. "Want some now, Trot?"

She shook her head, saying:

"That ought to keep us alive 'bout three days if we're careful of it."

"Longer'n that, Trot," said Cap'n Bill, but his voice was a little troubled and unsteady.

"But if we stay here we're bound to starve in time," continued the girl, "while if we go into th' dark hole —"

"Some things are more hard to face than starvation," said the sailor-man, gravely. "We don't know what's inside that dark hole. Trot, nor where it might lead us to."

"There's a way to find that out," she persisted.

Instead of replying, Cap'n Bill began searching in his pockets. He soon drew out a little package of fish-hooks and a long line. Trot watched him join them together. Then he crept a little way up the slope and turned over a big rock. Two or three small crabs began scurrying away over the sands and the old sailor caught them and put one on his hook and the others in his pocket. Coming back to the pool he swung the hook over his shoulder and circled it around his head and cast it nearly into the center of the water, where he allowed it to sink gradually, paying out the line as far as it would go. When the end was reached, he began drawing it in again, until the crab bait was floating on the surface.

Trot watched him cast the line a second time, and a third. She decided that either there were no fishes in the pool or they would not bite the crab bait. But Cap'n Bill was an old fisherman and not easily discouraged. When the crab got away he put another on the hook. When the crabs were all gone he climbed up the rocks and found some more.

Meantime Trot tired of watching him and lay down upon the sands, where she fell fast asleep. During the next two hours her clothing dried completely, as did that of the old sailor. They were both so used to salt water that there was no danger of taking cold.

Finally the little girl was wakened by a splash beside her and a grunt of satisfaction from Cap'n Bill. She opened her eyes to find that the Cap'n had landed a silver-scaled fish weighing about two pounds. This cheered her considerably and she hurried to scrape together a heap of seaweed, while Cap'n Bill cut up the fish with his jackknife and got it ready for cooking.

They had cooked fish with seaweed before. Cap'n Bill wrapped his fish in some of the weed and dipped it in the water to dampen it. Then he lighted a match and set fire to Trot's heap, which speedily burned down to a glowing bed of ashes. Then they laid the wrapped fish on the ashes, covered it with more seaweed, and allowed this to catch fire and burn to embers. After feeding the fire with seaweed for some time, the sailor finally decided that their supper was ready, so he scattered the ashes and drew out the bits of fish, still encased in their smoking wrappings. When these wrappings were removed, the fish was found thoroughly cooked and both Trot and Cap'n Bill ate of it freely. It had a slight flavor of seaweed and would have been better with a sprinkling of salt.

The soft glow which until now had lighted the cavern, began to grow dim, but there was a great quantity of seaweed in the place, so after they had eaten their fish they kept the fire alive for a time by giving it a handful of fuel now and then.

From an inner pocket the sailor drew a small flask of battered metal and unscrewing the cap handed it to Trot. She took but one swallow of the water, although she wanted more, and she noticed that Cap'n Bill merely wet his lips with it.

# Chapter Two

"S'pose," said she, staring at the glowing seaweed fire and speaking slowly, "that we can catch all the fish we need; how 'bout the drinking-water, Cap'n?"

He moved uneasily but did not reply. Both of them were thinking about the dark hole, but while Trot had little fear of it the old man could not overcome his dislike to enter the place. He knew that Trot was right, though. To remain in the cavern, where they now were, could only result in slow but sure death.

It was nighttime up on the earth's surface, so the little girl became drowsy and soon fell asleep. After a time the old sailor slumbered on the sands beside her. It was very still and nothing disturbed them for hours. When at last they awoke the cavern was light again.

They had divided one of the biscuits and were munching it for breakfast when they were startled by a sudden splash in the pool. Looking toward it they saw emerging from the water the most curious creature either of them had ever beheld. It wasn't a fish, Trot decided, nor was it a beast. It had wings, though, and queer wings they were: shaped like an inverted chopping-bowl and covered with tough skin instead of feathers. It had four legs — much like the legs of a stork, only double the number — and its head was shaped a good deal like that of a poll parrot, with a beak that curved downward in front and upward at the edges, and was half bill and half mouth. But to call it a bird was out of the question, because it had no feathers whatever except a crest of wavy plumes of a scarlet color on the very top of its head. The strange creature must have weighed as much as Cap'n Bill, and as it floundered and struggled to get out of the water to the sandy beach it was so big and unusual that both Trot and her companion stared at it in wonder — in wonder that was not unmixed with fear.

## CHAPTER 3

# The Ork

The eyes that regarded them, as the creature stood dripping before them, were bright and mild in expression, and the queer addition to their party made no attempt to attack them and seemed quite as surprised by the meeting as they were.

"I wonder," whispered Trot, "what it is."

"Who, me?" exclaimed the creature in a shrill, high-pitched voice. "Why, I'm an Ork."

"Oh!" said the girl. "But what is an Ork?"

"I am," he repeated, a little proudly, as he shook the water from his funny wings; "and if ever an Ork was glad to be out of the water and on dry land again,

33

you can be mighty sure that I'm that especial, individual Ork!"

"Have you been in the water long?" inquired Cap'n Bill, thinking it only polite to show an interest in the strange creature.

"Why, this last ducking was about ten minutes, I believe, and that's about nine minutes and sixty seconds too long for comfort," was the reply. "But last night I was in an awful pickle, I assure you. The whirlpool caught me, and — "

"Oh, were you in the whirlpool, too?" asked Trot eagerly.

He gave her a glance that was somewhat reproachful.

"I believe I was mentioning the fact, young lady, when your desire to talk interrupted me," said the Ork. "I am not usually careless in my actions, but that whirlpool was so busy yesterday that I thought I'd see what mischief it was up to. So I flew a little too near it and the suction of the air drew me down into the depths of the ocean. Water and I are natural enemies, and it would have conquered me this time had not a bevy of pretty mermaids come to my assistance and dragged me away from the whirling water and far up into a cavern, where they deserted me."

# Chapter Three

"Why, that's about the same thing that happened to us," cried Trot. "Was your cavern like this one?"

"I haven't examined this one yet," answered the Ork; "but if they happen to be alike I shudder at our fate, for the other one was a prison, with no outlet except by means of the water. I stayed there all night, however, and this morning I plunged into the pool, as far down as I could go, and then swam as hard and as far as I could. The rocks scraped my back, now and then, and I barely escaped the clutches of an ugly sea-monster; but by and by I came to the surface to catch my breath, and found myself here. That's the whole story, and as I see you have something to eat I entreat you to give me a share of it. The truth is, I'm half starved."

With these words the Ork squatted down beside them. Very reluctantly Cap'n Bill drew another biscuit from his pocket and held it out. The Ork promptly seized it in one of its front claws and began to nibble the biscuit in much the same manner a parrot might have done.

"We haven't much grub," said the sailor-man, "but we're willin' to share it with a comrade in distress."

"That's right," returned the Ork, cocking its head sidewise in a cheerful manner, and then for a few minutes there was silence while they all ate of the biscuits. After a while Trot said:

"I've never seen or heard of an Ork before. Are there many of you?"

"We are rather few and exclusive, I believe," was the reply. "In the country where I was born we are the absolute rulers of all living things, from ants to elephants."

"What country is that?" asked Cap'n Bill.

"Orkland."

"Where does it lie?"

"I don't know, exactly. You see, I have a restless nature, for some reason, while all the rest of my race are quiet and contented Orks and seldom stray far from home. From childhood days I loved to fly long distances away, although father often warned me that I would get into trouble by so doing.

"'It's a big world, Flipper, my son,' he would say, 'and I've heard that in parts of it live queer two-legged creatures called Men, who war upon all other living things and would have little respect for even an Ork.'

"This naturally aroused my curiosity and after I had completed my education and left school I decided to fly out into the world and try to get a glimpse of the creatures called Men. So I left home without saying good-bye, an act I shall always regret. Adventures were many, I found. I sighted men several times, but have never before been so close to them as now. Also I had to fight my way through the air, for I met gigantic birds, with fluffy feathers all over them, which attacked me fiercely. Besides, it kept me busy escaping from floating airships. In my rambling I had lost all track of distance or direction, so that when I wanted to go home I had no idea where my country was located. I've now been trying to find it for several months and it was during one of my flights over the ocean that I met the whirlpool and became its victim."

Trot and Cap'n Bill listened to this recital with much interest, and from the friendly tone and harmless appearance of the Ork they judged he was not likely to prove so disagreeable a companion as at first they had feared he might be.

The Ork sat upon its haunches much as a cat does, but used the finger-like claws of its front legs almost as cleverly as if they were hands. Perhaps the most curious thing about the creature was its tail, or what ought to have been its tail. This queer arrangement of skin, bones and muscle was shaped like the propellers used on boats and airships, having fan-like surfaces and being pivoted to its body. Cap'n Bill knew something of mechanics, and observing the propeller-like tail of the Ork he said:

"I s'pose you're a pretty swift flyer?"

"Yes, indeed; the Orks are admitted to be Kings of the Air."

"Your wings don't seem to amount to much," remarked Trot.

"Well, they are not very big," admitted the Ork, waving the four hollow skins gently to and fro, "but they serve to support my body in the air while I speed along by means of my tail. Still, taken altogether, I'm very handsomely formed, don't you think?"

Trot did not like to reply, but Cap'n Bill nodded gravely. "For an Ork," said he, "you're a wonder. I've never seen one afore, but I can imagine you're as good as any."

That seemed to please the creature and it began walking around the cavern, making its way easily up the slope. While it was gone, Trot and Cap'n Bill each took another sip from the water-flask, to wash down their breakfast.

"Why, here's a hole — an exit — an outlet!" exclaimed the Ork from above.

"We know," said Trot. "We found it last night."

"Well, then, let's be off," continued the Ork, after sticking its head into the black hole and sniffing once or twice. "The air seems fresh and sweet, and it can't lead us to any worse place than this."

The girl and the sailor-man got up and climbed to the side of the Ork.

"We'd about decided to explore this hole before you came," explained Cap'n Bill; "but it's a dangerous place to navigate in the dark, so wait till I light a candle."

"What is a candle?" inquired the Ork.

"You'll see in a minute," said Trot.

The old sailor drew one of the candles from his right-side pocket and the tin matchbox from his left-side pocket. When he lighted the match the Ork gave a startled jump and eyed the flame suspiciously; but Cap'n Bill proceeded to light the candle and the action interested the Ork very much.

"Light," it said, somewhat nervously, "is valuable in a hole of this sort. The candle is not dangerous, I hope?"

"Sometimes it burns your fingers," answered Trot, "but that's about the worst it can do — 'cept to blow out when you don't want it to."

Cap'n Bill shielded the flame with his hand and crept into the hole. It wasn't any too big for a grown man, but after he had crawled a few feet it grew larger. Trot came close behind him and then the Ork followed.

"Seems like a reg'lar tunnel," muttered the sailor-man, who was creeping along awkwardly because of his wooden leg. The rocks, too, hurt his knees.

For nearly half an hour the three moved slowly along the tunnel, which made many twists and turns and sometimes slanted downward and sometimes upward. Finally Cap'n Bill stopped short, with an exclamation of disappointment, and held the flickering candle far ahead to light the scene.

"What's wrong?" demanded Trot, who could see nothing because the sailor's form completely filled the hole.

"Why, we've come to the end of our travels, I guess," he replied.

"Is the hole blocked?" inquired the Ork.

"No; it's wuss nor that," replied Cap'n Bill sadly. "I'm on the edge of a precipice. Wait a minute an' I'll move along and let you see for yourselves. Be careful, Trot, not to fall."

Then he crept forward a little and moved to one side, holding the candle so that the girl could see to follow him. The Ork came next and now all three knelt on a narrow ledge of rock which dropped straight away and left a huge black space which the tiny flame of the candle could not illuminate.

"H-m!" said the Ork, peering over the edge; "this doesn't look very promising, I'll admit. But let me take your candle, and I'll fly down and see what's below us."

"Aren't you afraid?" asked Trot.

"Certainly I'm afraid," responded the Ork. "But

if we intend to escape we can't stay on this shelf forever. So, as I notice you poor creatures cannot fly, it is my duty to explore the place for you."

Cap'n Bill handed the Ork the candle, which had now burned to about half its length. The Ork took it in one claw rather cautiously and then tipped its body forward and slipped over the edge. They heard a queer buzzing sound, as the tail revolved, and a brisk flapping of the peculiar wings, but they were more interested just then in following with their eyes the tiny speck of light which marked the location of the candle. This light first made a great circle, then dropped slowly downward and suddenly was extinguished, leaving everything before them black as ink.

"Hi, there! How did that happen?" cried the Ork.

"It blew out, I guess," shouted Cap'n Bill. "Fetch it here."

"I can't see where you are," said the Ork.

So Cap'n Bill got out another candle and lighted it, and its flame enabled the Ork to fly back to them. It alighted on the edge and held out the bit of candle.

"What made it stop burning?" asked the creature.

"The wind," said Trot. "You must be more careful, this time."

"What's the place like?" inquired Cap'n Bill.

# Chapter Three

"I don't know, yet; but there must be a bottom to it, so I'll try to find it."

With this the Ork started out again and this time sank downward more slowly. Down, down, down it went, till the candle was a mere spark, and then it headed away to the left and Trot and Cap'n Bill lost all sight of it.

In a few minutes, however, they saw the spark of light again, and as the sailor still held the second lighted candle the Ork made straight toward them.

It was only a few yards distant when suddenly it dropped the candle with a cry of pain and next moment alighted, fluttering wildly, upon the rocky ledge.

"What's the matter?" asked Trot.

"It bit me!" wailed the Ork. "I don't like your candles. The thing began to disappear slowly as soon as I took it in my claw, and it grew smaller and smaller until just now it turned and bit me — a most unfriendly thing to do. Oh — oh! Ouch, what a bite!"

"That's the nature of candles, I'm sorry to say," explained Cap'n Bill, with a grin. "You have to handle 'em mighty keerful. But tell us, what did you find down there?"

"I found a way to continue our journey," said the Ork, nursing tenderly the claw which had been burned. "Just below us is a great lake of black water, which looked so cold and wicked that it made me shudder; but away at the left there's a big tunnel, which we can easily walk through. I don't know where it leads to, of course, but we must follow it and find out."

"Why, we can't get to it," protested the little girl. "We can't fly, as you do, you must remember."

"No, that's true," replied the Ork musingly.

"Your bodies are built very poorly, it seems to me, since all you can do is crawl upon the earth's surface. But you may ride upon my back, and in that way I can promise you a safe journey to the tunnel."

"Are you strong enough to carry us?" asked Cap'n Bill, doubtfully.

"Yes, indeed; I'm strong enough to carry a dozen of you, if you could find a place to sit," was the reply; "but there's only room between my wings for one at a time, so I'll have to make two trips."

"All right; I'll go first," decided Cap'n Bill.

He lit another candle for Trot to hold while they were gone and to light the Ork on his return to her, and then the old sailor got upon the Ork's back, where he sat with his wooden leg sticking straight out sidewise.

"If you start to fall, clasp your arms around my neck," advised the creature.

"If I start to fall, it's good night an' pleasant dreams," said Cap'n Bill.

"All ready?" asked the Ork.

"Start the buzz-tail," said Cap'n Bill, with a tremble in his voice. But the Ork flew away so gently that the old man never even tottered in his seat.

Trot watched the light of Cap'n Bill's candle till

it disappeared in the far distance. She didn't like to be left alone on this dangerous ledge, with a lake of black water hundreds of feet below her; but she was a brave little girl and waited patiently for the return of the Ork. It came even sooner than she had expected and the creature said to her:

" Your friend is safe in the tunnel. Now, then, get aboard and I'll carry you to him in a jiffy."

I'm sure not many little girls would have cared to take that awful ride through the huge black cavern on the back of a skinny Ork. Trot didn't care for it, herself, but it just had to be done and so she did it as courageously as possible. Her heart beat fast and she was so nervous she could scarcely hold the candle in her fingers as the Ork sped swiftly through the darkness.

It seemed like a long ride to her, yet in reality the Ork covered the distance in a wonderfully brief period of time and soon Trot stood safely beside Cap'n Bill on the level floor of a big arched tunnel. The sailor-man was very glad to greet his little comrade again and both were grateful to the Ork for his assistance.

"I dunno where this tunnel leads to," remarked Cap'n Bill, "but it surely looks more promisin' than that other hole we crept through."

# Chapter Three

"When the Ork is rested," said Trot, "we'll travel on and see what happens."

"Rested!" cried the Ork, as scornfully as his shrill voice would allow. "That bit of flying didn't tire me at all. I'm used to flying days at a time, without ever once stopping."

"Then let's move on," proposed Cap'n Bill. He still held in his hand one lighted candle, so Trot blew out the other flame and placed her candle in the sailor's big pocket. She knew it was not wise to burn two candles at once.

The tunnel was straight and smooth and very easy to walk through, so they made good progress. Trot thought that the tunnel began about two miles from the cavern where they had been cast by the whirlpool, but now it was impossible to guess the miles traveled, for they walked steadily for hours and hours without any change in their surroundings.

Finally Cap'n Bill stopped to rest.

"There's somethin' queer about this 'ere tunnel, I'm certain," he declared, wagging his head dolefully. "Here's three candles gone a'ready, an' only three more left us; yet the tunnel's the same as it was when we started. An' how long it's goin' to keep up, no one knows."

"Couldn't we walk without a light?" asked Trot. "The way seems safe enough."

"It does right now," was the reply, "but we can't tell when we are likely to come to another gulf, or somethin' jes' as dangerous. In that case we'd be killed afore we knew it."

"Suppose I go ahead?" suggested the Ork. "I don't fear a fall, you know, and if anything happens I'll call out and warn you."

"That's a good idea," declared Trot, and Cap'n Bill thought so, too. So the Ork started off ahead, quite in the dark, and hand in hand the two followed him.

When they had walked in this way for a good long time the Ork halted and demanded food. Cap'n Bill had not mentioned food because there was so little left — only three biscuits and a lump of cheese about as big as his two fingers — but he gave the Ork half of a biscuit, sighing as he did so. The creature didn't care for the cheese, so the sailor divided it between himself and Trot. They lighted a candle and sat down in the tunnel while they ate.

"My feet hurt me," grumbled the Ork. "I'm not used to walking and this rocky passage is so uneven and lumpy that it hurts me to walk upon it."

"Can't you fly along?" asked Trot.

# Chapter Three

"No; the roof is too low," said the Ork.

After the meal they resumed their journey, which Trot began to fear would never end. When Cap'n Bill noticed how tired the little girl was, he paused and lighted a match and looked at his big silver watch.

"Why, it's night!" he exclaimed. "We've tramped all day, an' still we're in this awful passage, which mebbe goes straight through the middle of the world, an' mebbe is a circle — in which case we can keep walkin' till doomsday. Not knowin' what's before us so well as we know what's behind us, I propose we make a stop, now, an' try to sleep till mornin'."

"That will suit me," asserted the Ork, with a groan. "My feet are hurting me dreadfully and for the last few miles I've been limping with pain."

"My foot hurts, too," said the sailor, looking for a smooth place on the rocky floor to sit down.

"*Your* foot!" cried the Ork. "Why, you've only one to hurt you, while I have four. So I suffer four times as much as you possibly can. Here; hold the candle while I look at the bottoms of my claws. I declare," he said, examining them by the flickering light, "there are bunches of pain all over them!"

"P'r'aps," said Trot, who was very glad to sit down beside her companions, "you've got corns."

"Corns? Nonsense! Orks never have corns," protested the creature, rubbing its sore feet tenderly.

"Then mebbe they're — they're — What do you call 'em, Cap'n Bill? Something 'bout the Pilgrim's Progress, you know."

"Bunions," said Cap'n Bill.

"Oh, yes; mebbe you've got bunions."

"It is possible," moaned the Ork. "But whatever they are, another day of such walking on them would drive me crazy."

"I'm sure they'll feel better by mornin'," said Cap'n Bill, encouragingly. "Go to sleep an' try to forget your sore feet."

The Ork cast a reproachful look at the sailor-man, who didn't see it. Then the creature asked plaintively: "Do we eat now, or do we starve?"

"There's only half a biscuit left for you," answered Cap'n Bill. "No one knows how long we'll have to stay in this dark tunnel, where there's nothing whatever to eat; so I advise you to save that morsel o' food till later."

"Give it me now!" demanded the Ork. "If I'm going to starve, I'll do it all at once — not by degrees."

Cap'n Bill produced the biscuit and the creature ate it in a trice. Trot was rather hungry and whispered to Cap'n Bill that she'd take part of her share; but the old man secretly broke his own half-biscuit in two, saving Trot's share for a time of greater need.

He was beginning to be worried over the little girl's plight and long after she was asleep and the Ork was snoring in a rather disagreeable manner, Cap'n Bill sat with his back to a rock and smoked his pipe and tried to think of some way to escape from this seemingly endless tunnel. But after a time he also slept, for hobbling on a wooden leg all day was tiresome, and there in the dark slumbered the three adventurers for many hours, until the Ork roused itself and kicked the old sailor with one foot.

"It must be another day," said he.

## CHAPTER 4

# Daylight at Last

Cap'n Bill rubbed his eyes, lit a match and consulted his watch.

"Nine o'clock. Yes, I guess it's another day, sure enough. Shall we go on?" he asked.

"Of course," replied the Ork. "Unless this tunnel is different from everything else in the world, and has no end, we'll find a way out of it sooner or later."

The sailor gently wakened Trot. She felt much rested by her long sleep and sprang to her feet eagerly.

"Let's start, Cap'n," was all she said.

They resumed the journey and had only taken a few steps when the Ork cried "Wow!" and made a great fluttering of its wings and whirling of its tail. The others, who were following a short distance behind, stopped abruptly.

"What's the matter?" asked Cap'n Bill.

"Give us a light," was the reply. "I think we've come to the end of the tunnel." Then, while Cap'n Bill lighted a candle, the creature added: "If that is true, we needn't have wakened so soon, for we were almost at the end of this place when we went to sleep."

The sailor-man and Trot came forward with a light. A wall of rock really faced the tunnel, but now they saw that the opening made a sharp turn to the left. So they followed on, by a narrower passage, and then made another sharp turn — this time to the right.

"Blow out the light, Cap'n," said the Ork, in a pleased voice. "We've struck daylight."

Daylight at last! A shaft of mellow light fell almost at their feet as Trot and the sailor turned the corner of the passage, but it came from above, and raising their eyes they found they were at the bottom of a deep, rocky well, with the top far, far above their heads. And here the passage ended.

For a while they gazed in silence, at least two of them being filled with dismay at the sight. But the Ork merely whistled softly and said cheerfully:

"That was the toughest journey I ever had the misfortune to undertake, and I'm glad it's over. Yet, unless I can manage to fly to the top of this pit, we are entombed here forever."

"Do you think there is room enough for you to fly in?" asked the little girl anxiously; and Cap'n Bill added:

"It's a straight-up shaft, so I don't see how you'll ever manage it."

"Were I an ordinary bird — one of those horrid feathered things — I wouldn't even make the attempt to fly out," said the Ork. "But my mechanical propeller tail can accomplish wonders, and whenever you're ready I'll show you a trick that is worth while."

"Oh!" exclaimed Trot; "do you intend to take us up, too?"

"Why not?"

"I thought," said Cap'n Bill, "as you'd go first, an' then send somebody to help us by lettin' down a rope."

"Ropes are dangerous," replied the Ork, "and I might not be able to find one to reach all this distance. Besides, it stands to reason that if I can get out myself I can also carry you two with me."

"Well, I'm not afraid," said Trot, who longed to be on the earth's surface again.

"S'pose we fall?" suggested Cap'n Bill, doubtfully.

"Why, in that case we would all fall together," returned the Ork. "Get aboard, little girl; sit across my shoulders and put both your arms around my neck."

Trot obeyed and when she was seated on the Ork, Cap'n Bill inquired:

"How 'bout me, Mr. Ork?"

"Why, I think you'd best grab hold of my rear legs and let me carry you up in that manner," was the reply.

Cap'n Bill looked way up at the top of the well, and then he looked at the Ork's slender, skinny legs and heaved a deep sigh.

"It's goin' to be some dangle, I guess; but if you don't waste too much time on the way up, I may be able to hang on," said he.

"All ready, then!" cried the Ork, and at once his whirling tail began to revolve. Trot felt herself rising into the air; when the creature's legs left the ground Cap'n Bill grasped two of them firmly and held on for dear life. The Ork's body was tipped straight upward, and Trot had to embrace the neck very tightly to keep from sliding off. Even in this position the Ork had trouble in escaping the rough sides of the well. Several times it exclaimed "Wow!" as it bumped its back, or a wing hit against some jagged projection; but the tail kept whirling with remarkable swiftness and the daylight grew brighter and brighter. It was, indeed, a long journey from the bottom to the top, yet almost before Trot realized they had come so far, they popped out of the hole into the clear air and sunshine and a moment later the Ork alighted gently upon the ground.

The release was so sudden that even with the crea-

ture's care for its passengers Cap'n Bill struck the earth with a shock that sent him rolling heel over head; but by the time Trot had slid down from her seat the old sailor-man was sitting up and looking around him with much satisfaction.

"It's sort o' pretty here," said he.

"Earth is a beautiful place!" cried Trot.

"I wonder where on earth we are?" pondered the Ork, turning first one bright eye and then the other to this side and that. Trees there were, in plenty,

and shrubs and flowers and green turf. But there were no houses; there were no paths; there was no sign of civilization whatever.

"Just before I settled down on the ground I thought I caught a view of the ocean," said the Ork. "Let's see if I was right." Then he flew to a little hill, near by, and Trot and Cap'n Bill followed him more slowly. When they stood on the top of the hill they could see the blue waves of the ocean in front of them, to the right of them, and at the left of them. Behind the hill was a forest that shut out the view.

"I hope it ain't an island, Trot," said Cap'n Bill gravely.

"If it is, I s'pose we're prisoners," she replied.

"Ezzackly so, Trot."

"But, even so, it's better than those terr'ble underground tunnels and caverns," declared the girl.

"You are right, little one," agreed the Ork. "Anything above ground is better than the best that lies under ground. So let's not quarrel with our fate but be thankful we've escaped."

"We are, indeed!" she replied. "But I wonder if we can find something to eat in this place?"

"Let's explore an' find out," proposed Cap'n Bill. "Those trees over at the left look like cherry-trees."

On the way to them the explorers had to walk through a tangle of vines and Cap'n Bill, who went first, stumbled and pitched forward on his face.

"Why, it's a melon!" cried Trot delightedly, as she saw what had caused the sailor to fall.

Cap'n Bill rose to his foot, for he was not at all hurt, and examined the melon. Then he took his big jackknife from his pocket and cut the melon open. It was quite ripe and looked delicious; but the old man tasted it before he permitted Trot to eat any. Deciding it was good he gave her a big slice and then offered the Ork some. The creature looked at the

59

fruit somewhat disdainfully, at first, but once he had tasted its flavor he ate of it as heartily as did the others. Among the vines they discovered many other melons, and Trot said gratefully: "Well, there's no danger of our starving, even if this *is* an island."

"Melons," remarked Cap'n Bill, "are both food an' water. We couldn't have struck anything better."

Farther on they came to the cherry trees, where they obtained some of the fruit, and at the edge of the little forest were wild plums. The forest itself consisted entirely of nut trees — walnuts, filberts, almonds and chestnuts — so there would be plenty of wholesome food for them while they remained there.

Cap'n Bill and Trot decided to walk through the forest, to discover what was on the other side of it, but the Ork's feet were still so sore and "lumpy" from walking on the rocks that the creature said he preferred to fly over the tree-tops and meet them on the other side. The forest was not large, so by walking briskly for fifteen minutes they reached its farthest edge and saw before them the shore of the ocean.

"It's an island, all right," said Trot, with a sigh.

"Yes, and a pretty island, too," said Cap'n Bill, trying to conceal his disappointment on Trot's account. "I guess, partner, if the wuss comes to the wuss,

I could build a raft — or even a boat — from those trees, so's we could sail away in it."

The little girl brightened at this suggestion.

"I don't see the Ork anywhere," she remarked, looking around. Then her eyes lighted upon something and she exclaimed: "Oh, Cap'n Bill! Isn't that a house, over there to the left?"

Cap'n Bill, looking closely, saw a shed-like structure built at one edge of the forest.

"Seems like it, Trot. Not that I'd call it much of a house, but it's a buildin', all right. Let's go over an' see if it's occypied."

## CHAPTER 5

# The Little Old Man of the Island

A few steps brought them to the shed, which was merely a roof of boughs built over a square space, with some branches of trees fastened to the sides to keep off the wind. The front was quite open and faced the sea, and as our friends came nearer they observed a little man, with a long pointed beard, sitting motionless on a stool and staring thoughtfully out over the water.

"Get out of the way, please," he called in a fretful voice. "Can't you see you are obstructing my view?"

"Good morning," said Cap'n Bill, politely.

"It isn't a good morning!" snapped the little man.

"I've seen plenty of mornings better than this. Do you call it a good morning when I'm pestered with such a crowd as you?"

Trot was astonished to hear such words from a stranger whom they had greeted quite properly, and Cap'n Bill grew red at the little man's rudeness. But the sailor said, in a quiet tone of voice:

"Are you the only one as lives on this 'ere island?"

"Your grammar's bad," was the reply. "But this is my own exclusive island, and I'll thank you to get off it as soon as possible."

"We'd like to do that," said Trot, and then she and Cap'n Bill turned away and walked down to the shore, to see if any other land was in sight.

The little man rose and followed them, although both were now too provoked to pay any attention to him.

"Nothin' in sight, partner," reported Cap'n Bill, shading his eyes with his hand; "so we'll have to stay here for a time, anyhow. It isn't a bad place, Trot, by any means."

"That's all you know about it!" broke in the little man. "The trees are altogether too green and the rocks are harder than they ought to be. I find the sand very grainy and the water dreadfully wet.

Every breeze makes a draught and the sun shines in the daytime, when there's no need of it, and disappears just as soon as it begins to get dark. If you remain here you'll find the island very unsatisfactory."

Trot turned to look at him, and her sweet face was grave and curious.

"I wonder who you are," she said.

"My name is Pessim," said he, with an air of pride. "I'm called the Observer."

"Oh. What do you observe?" asked the little girl.

"Everything I see," was the reply, in a more surly tone. Then Pessim drew back with a startled exclamation and looked at some footprints in the sand. "Why, good gracious me!" he cried in distress.

"What's the matter now?" asked Cap'n Bill.

"Someone has pushed the earth in! Don't you see it?"

"It isn't pushed in far enough to hurt anything," said Trot, examining the footprints.

"Everything hurts that isn't right," insisted the man. "If the earth were pushed in a mile, it would be a great calamity, wouldn't it?"

"I s'pose so," admitted the little girl.

"Well, here it is pushed in a full inch! That's a twelfth of a foot, or a little more than a millionth part of a mile. Therefore it is one-millionth part of a calamity — Oh, dear! How dreadful!" said Pessim in a wailing voice.

"Try to forget it, sir," advised Cap'n Bill, soothingly. "It's beginning to rain. Let's get under your shed and keep dry."

"Raining! Is it really raining?" asked Pessim, beginning to weep.

"It is," answered Cap'n Bill, as the drops began to descend, "and I don't see any way to stop it — although I'm some observer myself."

"No; we can't stop it, I fear," said the man. "Are you very busy just now?"

"I won't be after I get to the shed," replied the sailor-man.

"Then do me a favor, please," begged Pessim, walking briskly along behind them, for they were hastening to the shed.

"Depends on what it is," said Cap'n Bill.

"I wish you would take my umbrella down to the shore and hold it over the poor fishes till it stops raining. I'm afraid they'll get wet," said Pessim.

Trot laughed, but Cap'n Bill thought the little man was poking fun at him and so he scowled upon Pessim in a way that showed he was angry.

# The Scarecrow of Oz

They reached the shed before getting very wet, although the rain was now coming down in big drops. The roof of the shed protected them and while they stood watching the rainstorm something buzzed in and circled around Pessim's head. At once the Observer began beating it away with his hands, crying out:

"A bumblebee! A bumblebee! The queerest bumblebee I ever saw!"

Cap'n Bill and Trot both looked at it and the little girl said in surprise:

"Dear me! It's a wee little Ork!"

"That's what it is, sure enough," exclaimed Cap'n Bill.

Really, it wasn't much bigger than a big bumblebee, and when it came toward Trot she allowed it to alight on her shoulder.

"It's me, all right," said a very small voice in her ear; "but I'm in an awful pickle, just the same!"

"What, are you *our* Ork, then?" demanded the girl, much amazed.

"No, I'm my own Ork. But I'm the only Ork you know," replied the tiny creature.

"What's happened to you?" asked the sailor, putting his head close to Trot's shoulder in order to hear the reply better. Pessim also put his head close, and the Ork said:

"You will remember that when I left you I started to fly over the trees, and just as I got to this side of the forest I saw a bush that was loaded down

with the most luscious fruit you can imagine. The fruit was about the size of a gooseberry and of a lovely lavender color. So I swooped down and picked off one in my bill and ate it. At once I began to grow small. I could feel myself shrinking, shrinking away, and it frightened me terribly, so that I alighted on the ground to think over what was happening. In a few seconds I had shrunk to the size you now see me; but there I remained, getting no smaller, indeed, but no larger. It is certainly a dreadful affliction! After I had recovered somewhat from the shock I began to search for you. It is not so easy to find one's way when a creature is so small, but fortunately I spied you here in this shed and came to you at once."

Cap'n Bill and Trot were much astonished at this story and felt grieved for the poor Ork, but the little man Pessim seemed to think it a good joke. He began laughing when he heard the story and laughed until he choked, after which he lay down on the ground and rolled and laughed again, while the tears of merriment coursed down his wrinkled cheeks.

"Oh, dear! Oh, dear!" he finally gasped, sitting up and wiping his eyes. "This is too rich! It's almost too joyful to be true."

"I don't see anything funny about it," remarked Trot indignantly.

"You would if you'd had my experience," said Pessim, getting upon his feet and gradually resuming his solemn and dissatisfied expression of countenance. "The same thing happened to me."

# Chapter Five

"Oh, did it? And how did you happen to come to this island?" asked the girl.

"I didn't come; the neighbors brought me," replied the little man, with a frown at the recollection. "They said I was quarrelsome and fault-finding and blamed me because I told them all the things that went wrong, or never were right, and because I told them how things ought to be. So they brought me here and left me all alone, saying that if I quarreled with myself, no one else would be made unhappy. Absurd, wasn't it?"

"Seems to me," said Cap'n Bill, "those neighbors did the proper thing."

"Well," resumed Pessim, "when I found myself King of this island I was obliged to live upon fruits, and I found many fruits growing here that I had never seen before. I tasted several and found them good and wholesome. But one day I ate a lavender berry — as the Ork did — and immediately I grew so small that I was scarcely two inches high. It was a very unpleasant condition and like the Ork I became frightened. I could not walk very well nor very far, for every lump of earth in my way seemed a mountain, every blade of grass a tree and every grain of sand a rocky boulder. For several days I stumbled around in an agony of fear. Once a tree toad nearly gobbled me up, and if I ran out from the shelter of the bushes the gulls and cormorants swooped down upon me. Finally I decided to eat another berry and become nothing at all, since life, to one as small as I was, had become a dreary nightmare.

"At last I found a small tree that I thought bore the same fruit as that I had eaten. The berry was dark purple instead of light lavender, but otherwise it was quite similar. Being unable to climb the tree, I was obliged to wait underneath it until a sharp breeze arose and shook the limbs so that a berry fell. Instantly I seized it and taking a last view of the world — as I then thought — I ate the berry in a twinkling. Then, to my surprise, I began to grow big again, until I became of my former stature, and so I have since remained. Needless to say, I have never eaten again of the lavender fruit, nor do any of the beasts or birds that live upon this island eat it."

They had all three listened eagerly to this amazing tale, and when it was finished the Ork exclaimed:

"Do you think, then, that the deep purple berry is the antidote for the lavender one?"

"I'm sure of it," answered Pessim.

"Then lead me to the tree at once!" begged the Ork, "for this tiny form I now have terrifies me greatly."

Pessim examined the Ork closely.

"You are ugly enough as you are," said he. "Were you any larger you might be dangerous."

"Oh, no," Trot assured him; "the Ork has been our good friend. Please take us to the tree."

Then Pessim consented, although rather reluctantly. He led them to the right, which was the east side of the island, and in a few minutes brought them near to the edge of the grove which faced the shore of the ocean. Here stood a small tree bearing berries of a deep purple color. The fruit looked very enticing and Cap'n Bill reached up and selected one that seemed especially plump and ripe.

The Ork had remained perched upon Trot's shoulder but now it flew down to the ground. It was so difficult for Cap'n Bill to kneel down, with his wooden leg, that the little girl took the berry from him and held it close to the Ork's head.

"It's too big to go into my mouth," said the little creature, looking at the fruit sidewise.

"You'll have to make sev'ral mouthfuls of it, I guess," said Trot; and that is what the Ork did. He pecked at the soft, ripe fruit with his bill and ate it up very quickly, because it was good.

Even before he had finished the berry they could see the Ork begin to grow. In a few minutes he had regained his natural size and was strutting before them, quite delighted with his transformation.

"Well, well! What do you think of me now?" he asked proudly.

"You are very skinny and remarkably ugly," declared Pessim.

"You are a poor judge of Orks," was the reply. "Anyone can see that I'm much handsomer than those dreadful things called birds, which are all fluff and feathers."

"Their feathers make soft beds," asserted Pessim.

"And my skin would make excellent drumheads," retorted the Ork. "Nevertheless, a plucked bird or a skinned Ork would be of no value to himself, so we needn't brag of our usefulness after we are dead. But for the sake of argument, friend Pessim, I'd like to know what good *you* would be, were you not alive?"

"Never mind that," said Cap'n Bill. "He isn't much good as he is."

"I am King of this Island, allow me to say, and you're intruding on my property," declared the little man, scowling upon them. "If you don't like me — and I'm sure you don't, for no one else does — why don't you go away and leave me to myself?"

"Well, the Ork can fly, but we can't," explained Trot, in answer. "We don't want to stay here a bit, but I don't see how we can get away."

"You can go back into the hole you came from."

Cap'n Bill shook his head; Trot shuddered at the thought; the Ork laughed aloud.

"You may be King here," the creature said to Pessim, "but we intend to run this island to suit ourselves, for we are three and you are one, and the balance of power lies with us."

The little man made no reply to this, although as they walked back to the shed his face wore its fiercest scowl. Cap'n Bill gathered a lot of leaves and, assisted by Trot, prepared two nice beds in opposite corners of the shed. Pessim slept in a hammock which he swung between two trees.

They required no dishes, as all their food consisted of fruits and nuts picked from the trees; they made no fire, for the weather was warm and there was nothing to cook; the shed had no furniture other than the rude stool which the little man was accustomed to sit upon. He called it his " throne " and they let him keep it.

So they lived upon the island for three days, and rested and ate to their hearts' content. Still, they were not at all happy in this life because of Pessim. He continually found fault with them, and all that they did, and all their surroundings. He could see nothing good or admirable in all the world and Trot soon came to understand why the little man's former neighbors had brought him to this island and left him there, all alone, so he could not annoy anyone. It was their misfortune that they had been led to this place by their adventures, for often they would have preferred the company of a wild beast to that of Pessim.

On the fourth day a happy thought came to the Ork. They had all been racking their brains for a possible way to leave the island, and discussing this or that method, without finding a plan that was practical. Cap'n Bill had said he could make a raft of the trees, big enough to float them all, but he had no tools except those two pocketknives and it was not possible to chop down trees with such small blades.

"And s'pose we got afloat on the ocean," said Trot, "where would we drift to, and how long would it take us to get there?"

Cap'n Bill was forced to admit he didn't know. The Ork could fly away from the island any time it wished to, but the queer creature was loyal to his new friends and refused to leave them in such a lonely, forsaken place.

It was when Trot urged him to go, on this fourth morning, that the Ork had his happy thought.

"I will go," said he, "if you two will agree to ride upon my back."

"We are too heavy; you might drop us," objected Cap'n Bill.

"Yes, you are rather heavy for a long journey," acknowledged the Ork, "but you might eat of those lavender berries and become so small that I could carry you with ease."

This quaint suggestion startled Trot and she looked gravely at the speaker while she considered it, but Cap'n Bill gave a scornful snort and asked:

"What would become of us afterward? We wouldn't be much good if we were some two or three inches high. No, Mr. Ork, I'd rather stay here, as I am, than be a hop-o'-my-thumb somewhere else."

"Why couldn't you take some of the dark purple berries along with you, to eat after we had reached our destination?" inquired the Ork. "Then you could grow big again whenever you pleased."

Trot clapped her hands with delight.

"That's it!" she exclaimed. "Let's do it, Cap'n Bill."

The old sailor did not like the idea at first, but he thought it over carefully and the more he thought the better it seemed.

"How could you manage to carry us, if we were so small?" he asked.

"I could put you in a paper bag, and tie the bag around my neck."

"But we haven't a paper bag," objected Trot.
The Ork looked at her.

"There's your sunbonnet," it said presently, "which is hollow in the middle and has two strings that you could tie around my neck."

Trot took off her sunbonnet and regarded it critically. Yes, it might easily hold both her and Cap'n Bill, after they had eaten the lavender berries and been reduced in size. She tied the strings around the Ork's neck and the sunbonnet made a bag in which two tiny people might ride without danger of falling out. So she said:

"I b'lieve we'll do it that way, Cap'n."

Cap'n Bill groaned but could make no logical objection except that the plan seemed to him quite dangerous — and dangerous in more ways than one.

"I think so, myself," said Trot soberly. "But nobody can stay alive without getting into danger sometimes, and danger doesn't mean getting hurt, Cap'n; it only means we *might* get hurt. So I guess we'll have to take the risk."

"Let's go and find the berries," said the Ork.

They said nothing to Pessim, who was sitting on his stool and scowling dismally as he stared at the ocean, but started at once to seek the trees that bore the magic fruits. The Ork remembered very well where the lavender berries grew and led his companions quickly to the spot.

Cap'n Bill gathered two berries and placed them carefully in his pocket. Then they went around to the east side of the island and found the tree that bore the dark purple berries.

"I guess I'll take four of these," said the sailor-man, "so in case one doesn't make us grow big we can eat another."

"Better take six," advised the Ork. "It's well to be on the safe side, and I'm sure these trees grow nowhere else in all the world."

So Cap'n Bill gathered six of the purple berries and with their precious fruit they returned to the shed to big good-bye to Pessim. Perhaps they would not have granted the surly little man this courtesy had they not wished to use him to tie the sunbonnet around the Ork's neck.

When Pessim learned they were about to leave him he at first looked greatly pleased, but he suddenly recollected that nothing ought to please him and so began to grumble about being left alone.

"We knew it wouldn't suit you," remarked Cap'n Bill. "It didn't suit you to have us here, and it won't suit you to have us go away."

"That is quite true," admitted Pessim. "I haven't been suited since I can remember; so it doesn't matter to me in the least whether you go or stay."

He was interested in their experiment, however, and willingly agreed to assist, although he prophesied they would fall out of the sunbonnet on their way and be either drowned in the ocean or crushed upon some rocky shore. This uncheerful prospect did not daunt Trot, but it made Cap'n Bill quite nervous.

"I will eat my berry first," said Trot, as she placed her sunbonnet on the ground, in such manner that they could get into it.

Then she ate the lavender berry and in a few seconds became so small that Cap'n Bill picked her up gently with his thumb and one finger and placed her in the middle of the sunbonnet. Then he placed beside her the six purple berries — each one being about as big as the tiny Trot's head — and all preparations being now made the old sailor ate his lavender berry and became very small — wooden leg and all!

Cap'n Bill stumbled sadly in trying to climb over the edge of the sunbonnet and pitched in beside Trot headfirst, which caused the unhappy Pessim to laugh with glee. Then the King of the Island picked up the sunbonnet — so rudely that he shook its occupants like peas in a pod — and tied it, by means of its strings, securely around the Ork's neck.

"I hope, Trot, you sewed those strings on tight," said Cap'n Bill anxiously.

"Why, we are not very heavy, you know," she replied, "so I think the stitches will hold. But be careful and not crush the berries, Cap'n."

"One is jammed already," he said, looking at them.

"All ready?" asked the Ork.

" Yes! " they cried together, and Pessim came close to the sunbonnet and called out to them: " You'll be smashed or drowned, I'm sure you will! But farewell, and good riddance to you."

The Ork was provoked by this unkind speech, so he turned his tail toward the little man and made it revolve so fast that the rush of air tumbled Pessim over backward and he rolled several times upon the ground before he could stop himself and sit up. By that time the Ork was high in the air and speeding swiftly over the ocean.

## CHAPTER 6

# The Flight of the Midgets

Cap'n Bill and Trot rode very comfortably in the sunbonnet. The motion was quite steady, for they weighed so little that the Ork flew without effort. Yet they were both somewhat nervous about their future fate and could not help wishing they were safe on land and their natural size again.

"You're terr'ble small, Trot," remarked Cap'n Bill, looking at his companion.

"Same to you, Cap'n," she said with a laugh; "but as long as we have the purple berries we needn't worry about our size."

"In a circus," mused the old man, "we'd be curiosities. But in a sunbonnet — high up in the air — sailin' over a big, unknown ocean — they ain't no word in any booktionary to describe us."

"Why, we're midgets, that's all," said the little girl.

The Ork flew silently for a long time. The slight swaying of the sunbonnet made Cap'n Bill drowsy, and he began to doze. Trot, however, was wide awake, and after enduring the monotonous journey as long as she was able she called out:

"Don't you see land anywhere, Mr. Ork?"

"Not yet," he answered. "This is a big ocean and I've no idea in which direction the nearest land to that island lies; but if I keep flying in a straight line I'm sure to reach some place some time."

That seemed reasonable, so the little people in the sunbonnet remained as patient as possible; that is, Cap'n Bill dozed and Trot tried to remember her geography lessons so she could figure out what land they were likely to arrive at.

For hours and hours the Ork flew steadily, keeping to the straight line and searching with his eyes the horizon of the ocean for land. Cap'n Bill was fast asleep and snoring and Trot had laid her head on his shoulder to rest it when suddenly the Ork exclaimed:

"There! I've caught a glimpse of land, at last."

At this announcement they roused themselves. Cap'n Bill stood up and tried to peek over the edge of the sunbonnet.

"What does it look like?" he inquired.

"Looks like another island," said the Ork; "but I can judge it better in a minute or two."

"I don't care much for islands, since we visited that other one," declared Trot.

Soon the Ork made another announcement.

"It is surely an island, and a little one, too," said he. "But I won't stop, because I see a much bigger land straight ahead of it."

"That's right," approved Cap'n Bill. "The bigger the land, the better it will suit us."

"It's almost a continent," continued the Ork after a brief silence, during which he did not decrease the speed of his flight. "I wonder if it can be Orkland, the place I have been seeking so long?"

"I hope not," whispered Trot to Cap'n Bill — so softly that the Ork could not hear her — "for I shouldn't like to be in a country where only Orks live. This one Ork isn't a bad companion, but a lot of him wouldn't be much fun."

After a few more minutes of flying the Ork called out in a sad voice:

"No! this is not my country. It's a place I have never seen before, although I have wandered far and wide. It seems to be all mountains and deserts and green valleys and queer cities and lakes and rivers — mixed up in a very puzzling way."

"Most countries are like that," commented Cap'n Bill. "Are you going to land?"

"Pretty soon," was the reply. "There is a mountain peak just ahead of me. What do you say to our landing on that?"

"All right," agreed the sailor-man, for both he and Trot were getting tired of riding in the sunbonnet and longed to set foot on solid ground again.

So in a few minutes the Ork slowed down his speed and then came to a stop so easily that they were scarcely jarred at all. Then the creature squatted down until the sunbonnet rested on the ground, and began trying to unfasten with its claws the knotted strings.

This proved a very clumsy task, because the strings were tied at the back of the Ork's neck, just where his claws would not easily reach. After much fumbling he said:

"I'm afraid I can't let you out, and there is no one near to help me."

This was at first discouraging, but after a little thought Cap'n Bill said:

"If you don't mind, Trot, I can cut a slit in your sunbonnet with my knife."

"Do," she replied. "The slit won't matter, 'cause I can sew it up again afterward, when I am big."

So Cap'n Bill got out his knife, which was just as small, in proportion, as he was, and after considerable trouble managed to cut a long slit in the sunbonnet. First he squeezed through the opening himself and then helped Trot to get out.

When they stood on firm ground again their first act was to begin eating the dark purple berries which they had brought with them. Two of these Trot had guarded carefully during the long journey, by holding them in her lap, for their safety meant much to the tiny people.

"I'm not very hungry," said the little girl as she handed a berry to Cap'n Bill, "but hunger doesn't count, in this case. It's like taking medicine to make you well, so we must manage to eat 'em, somehow or other."

But the berries proved quite pleasant to taste and as Cap'n Bill and Trot nibbled at their edges their forms began to grow in size — slowly but steadily. The bigger they grew the easier it was for them to eat the berries, which of course became smaller to them, and by the time the fruit was eaten our friends had regained their natural size.

The little girl was greatly relieved when she found herself as large as she had ever been, and Cap'n Bill shared her satisfaction; for, although they had seen the effect of the berries on the Ork, they had not been sure the magic fruit would have the same effect on human beings, or that the magic would work in any other country than that in which the berries grew.

"What shall we do with the other four berries?" asked Trot, as she picked up her sunbonnet, marveling that she had ever been small enough to ride in it. "They're no good to us now, are they, Cap'n?"

"I'm not sure as to that," he replied. "If they were eaten by one who had never eaten the lavender berries, they might have no effect at all; but then, contrarywise, they might. One of 'em has got badly jammed, so I'll throw it away, but the other three I b'lieve I'll carry with me. They're magic things, you know, and may come handy to us some time."

He now searched in his big pockets and drew out a small wooden box with a sliding cover. The sailor had kept an assortment of nails, of various sizes, in this box, but those he now dumped loosely into his pocket and in the box placed the three sound purple berries.

When this important matter was attended to they found time to look about them and see what sort of place the Ork had landed them in.

## CHAPTER 7

# The Bumpy Man

The mountain on which they had alighted was not a barren waste, but had on its sides patches of green grass, some bushes, a few slender trees and here and there masses of tumbled rocks. The sides of the slope seemed rather steep, but with care one could climb up or down them with ease and safety. The view from where they now stood showed pleasant valleys and fertile hills lying below the heights. Trot thought she saw some houses of queer shapes scattered about the lower landscape, and there were moving dots that might be people or animals, yet were too far away for her to see them clearly.

Not far from the place where they stood was the top of the mountain, which seemed to be flat, so the Ork proposed to his companions that he would fly up and see what was there.

"That's a good idea," said Trot, "'cause it's getting toward evening and we'll have to find a place to sleep."

The Ork had not been gone more than a few minutes when they saw him appear on the edge of the top which was nearest them.

"Come on up!" he called.

So Trot and Cap'n Bill began to ascend the steep slope and it did not take them long to reach the place where the Ork awaited them.

Their first view of the mountain top pleased them very much. It was a level space of wider extent than they had guessed and upon it grew grass of a brilliant green color. In the very center stood a house built of stone and very neatly constructed. No one was in sight, but smoke was coming from the chimney, so with one accord all three began walking toward the house.

"I wonder," said Trot, "in what country we are, and if it's very far from my home in California."

"Can't say as to that, partner," answered Cap'n

Bill, "but I'm mighty certain we've come a long way since we struck that whirlpool."

"Yes," she agreed, with a sigh, "it must be miles and miles!"

"Distance means nothing," said the Ork. "I have flown pretty much all over the world, trying to find my home, and it is astonishing how many little countries there are, hidden away in the cracks and corners of this big globe of Earth. If one travels, he may find some new country at every turn, and a good many of them have never yet been put upon the maps."

"P'raps this is one of them," suggested Trot.

They reached the house after a brisk walk and Cap'n Bill knocked upon the door. It was at once opened by a rugged looking man who had "bumps all over him," as Trot afterward declared. There were bumps on his head, bumps on his body and bumps on his arms and legs and hands. Even his fingers had bumps on the ends of them. For dress he wore an old gray suit of fantastic design, which fitted him very badly because of the bumps it covered but could not conceal.

But the Bumpy Man's eyes were kind and twinkling in expression and as soon as he saw his visitors he bowed low and said in a rather bumpy voice:

"Happy day! Come in and shut the door, for it

grows cool when the sun goes down. Winter is now upon us."

"Why, it isn't cold a bit, outside," said Trot, "so it can't be winter yet."

"You will change your mind about that in a little while," declared the Bumpy Man. "My bumps always tell me the state of the weather, and they feel just now as if a snowstorm was coming this way. But make yourselves at home, strangers. Supper is nearly ready and there is food enough for all."

Inside the house there was but one large room, simply but comfortably furnished. It had benches, a table and a fireplace, all made of stone. On the hearth a pot was bubbling and steaming, and Trot thought it had a rather nice smell. The visitors seated themselves upon the benches — except the Ork. which squatted by the fireplace — and the Bumpy Man began stirring the kettle briskly.

"May I ask what country this is, sir?" inquired Cap'n Bill.

"Goodness me — fruit-cake and apple-sauce! — don't you know where you are?" asked the Bumpy Man, as he stopped stirring and looked at the speaker in surprise.

"No," admitted Cap'n Bill. "We've just arrived."

"Lost your way?" questioned the Bumpy Man.

"Not exactly," said Cap'n Bill. "We didn't have any way to lose."

"Ah!" said the Bumpy Man, nodding his bumpy head. "This," he announced, in a solemn, impressive voice, "is the famous Land of Mo."

"Oh!" exclaimed the sailor and the girl, both in one breath. But, never having heard of the Land of Mo, they were no wiser than before.

"I thought that would startle you," remarked the Bumpy Man, well pleased, as he resumed his stirring. The Ork watched him a while in silence and then asked:

"Who may *you* be?"

"Me?" answered the Bumpy Man. "Haven't you heard of me? Gingerbread and lemon-juice! I'm known, far and wide, as the Mountain Ear."

They all received this information in silence at first, for they were trying to think what he could mean. Finally Trot mustered up courage to ask:

"What is a Mountain Ear, please?"

For answer the man turned around and faced them, waving the spoon with which he had been stirring the kettle, as he recited the following verses in a singsong tone of voice:

" Here's a mountain, hard of hearing,
  That's sad-hearted and needs cheering,
So my duty is to listen to all sounds that Nature makes,
  So the hill won't get uneasy —
  Get to coughing, or get sneezy —
For this monster bump, when frightened, is quite
    liable to quakes.


" *You* can hear a bell that's ringing;
  *I* can feel some people's singing;
But a mountain isn't sensible of what goes on, and so
  When I hear a blizzard blowing
  Or it's raining hard, or snowing,
I tell it to the mountain and the mountain seems to
    know.


" Thus I benefit all people
  While I'm living on this steeple,
For I keep the mountain steady so my neighbors all
    may thrive.
  With my list'ning and my shouting
  I prevent this mount from spouting,
And that makes me so important that I'm glad that
    I'm alive."

# Chapter Seven

When he had finished these lines of verse the Bumpy Man turned again to resume his stirring. The Ork laughed softly and Cap'n Bill whistled to himself and Trot made up her mind that the Mountain Ear must be a little crazy. But the Bumpy Man seemed satisfied that he had explained his position fully and presently he placed four stone plates upon the table and then lifted the kettle from the fire and poured some of its contents on each of the plates. Cap'n Bill and Trot at once approached the table, for they were hungry, but when she examined her plate the little girl exclaimed:

" Why, it's molasses candy! "

"To be sure," returned the Bumpy Man, with a pleasant smile. " Eat it quick, while it's hot, for it cools very quickly this winter weather."

With this he seized a stone spoon and began putting the hot molasses candy into his mouth, while the others watched him in astonishment.

" Doesn't it burn you? " asked the girl.

" No indeed," said he. " Why don't you eat? Aren't you hungry? "

" Yes," she replied, " I am hungry. But we usually eat our candy when it is cold and hard. We always pull molasses candy before we eat it."

"Ha, ha, ha!" laughed the Mountain Ear. "What a funny idea! Where in the world did you come from?"

"California," she said.

"California! Pooh! there isn't any such place. I've heard of every place in the Land of Mo, but I never before heard of California."

" It isn't in the Land of Mo," she explained.

" Then it isn't worth talking about," declared the Bumpy Man, helping himself again from the steaming kettle, for he had been eating all the time he talked.

" For my part," sighed Cap'n Bill, " I'd like a decent square meal, once more, just by way of variety. In

the last place there was nothing but fruit to eat, and here it's worse, for there's nothing but candy."

"Molasses candy isn't so bad," said Trot. "Mine's nearly cool enough to pull, already. Wait a bit, Cap'n, and you can eat it."

A little later she was able to gather the candy from the stone plate and begin to work it back and forth with her hands. The Mountain Ear was greatly amazed at this and watched her closely. It was really good candy and pulled beautifully, so that Trot was soon ready to cut it into chunks for eating.

Cap'n Bill condescended to eat one or two pieces and the Ork ate several, but the Bumpy Man refused to try it. Trot finished the plate of candy herself and then asked for a drink of water.

"Water?" said the Mountain Ear wonderingly. "What is that?"

"Something to drink. Don't you have water in Mo?"

"None that ever I heard of," said he. "But I can give you some fresh lemonade. I caught it in a jar the last time it rained, which was only day before yesterday."

"Oh, does it rain lemonade here?" she inquired.

"Always; and it is very refreshing and healthful."

With this he brought from a cupboard a stone jar and a dipper, and the girl found it very nice lemonade, indeed. Cap'n Bill liked it, too; but the Ork would not touch it.

"If there is no water in this country, I cannot stay here for long," the creature declared. "Water means life to man and beast and bird."

"There must be water in lemonade," said Trot.

"Yes," answered the Ork, "I suppose so; but there are other things in it, too, and they spoil the good water."

The day's adventures had made our wanderers tired, so the Bumpy Man brought them some blankets in which they rolled themselves and then lay down before the fire, which their host kept alive with fuel all through the night. Trot wakened several times and found the Mountain Ear always alert and listening intently for the slightest sound. But the little girl could hear no sound at all except the snores of Cap'n Bill.

## CHAPTER 8

# Button-Bright is Lost and Found Again

"Wake up — wake up!" called the voice of the Bumpy Man. "Didn't I tell you winter was coming? I could hear it coming with my left ear, and the proof is that it is now snowing hard outside."

"Is it?" said Trot, rubbing her eyes and creeping out of her blanket. "Where I live, in California, I have never seen snow, except far away on the tops of high mountains."

"Well, this is the top of a high mountain," returned the bumpy one, "and for that reason we get our heaviest snowfalls right here."

The little girl went to the window and looked out.

The air was filled with falling white flakes, so large in size and so queer in form that she was puzzled.

"Are you certain this is snow?" she asked.

"To be sure. I must get my snow-shovel and turn out to shovel a path. Would you like to come with me?"

"Yes," she said, and followed the Bumpy Man out when he opened the door. Then she exclaimed: "Why, it isn't cold a bit!"

"Of course not," replied the man. "It was cold last night, before the snowstorm; but snow, when it falls, is alway crisp and warm."

Trot gathered a handful of it.

"Why, it's popcorn?" she cried.

"Certainly; all snow is popcorn. What did you expect it to be?"

"Popcorn is not snow in my country."

"Well, it is the only snow we have in the Land of Mo, so you may as well make the best of it," said he, a little impatiently. "I'm not responsible for the absurd things that happen in your country, and when you're in Mo you must do as the Momen do. Eat some of our snow, and you will find it is good. The only fault I find with our snow is that we get too much of it at times."

# Chapter Eight

With this the Bumpy Man set to work shoveling a path and he was so quick and industrious that he piled up the popcorn in great banks on either side of the trail that led to the mountain-top from the plains below. While he worked, Trot ate popcorn and found it crisp and slightly warm, as well as nicely salted and buttered. Presently Cap'n Bill came out of the house and joined her.

"What's this?" he asked.

"Mo snow," said she. "But it isn't real snow, although it falls from the sky. It's popcorn."

Cap'n Bill tasted it; then he sat down in the path and began to eat. The Ork came out and pecked away with its bill as fast as it could. They all liked popcorn and they all were hungry this morning.

Meantime the flakes of "Mo snow" came down so fast that the number of them almost darkened the air. The Bumpy Man was now shoveling quite a distance down the mountain-side, while the path behind him rapidly filled up with fresh-fallen popcorn. Suddenly Trot heard him call out:

"Goodness gracious — mince pie and pancakes! — here is some one buried in the snow."

She ran toward him at once and the others followed, wading through the corn and crunching it underneath their feet. The Mo snow was pretty deep where the Bumpy Man was shoveling and from beneath a great bank of it he had uncovered a pair of feet.

"Dear me! Someone has been lost in the storm," said Cap'n Bill. "I hope he is still alive. Let's pull him out and see."

He took hold of one foot and the Bumpy Man took hold of the other. Then they both pulled and out from the heap of popcorn came a little boy. He was dressed in a brown velvet jacket and knickerbockers, with brown stockings, buckled shoes and a blue shirt-waist that had frills down its front. When drawn from the heap the boy was chewing a mouthful of popcorn and both his hands were full of it. So at first he couldn't speak to his rescuers but lay quite still and eyed them calmly until he had swallowed his mouthful. Then he said:

"Get my cap," and stuffed more popcorn into his mouth.

While the Bumpy Man began shoveling into the corn-bank to find the boy's cap, Trot was laughing joyfully and Cap'n Bill had a broad grin on his face. The Ork looked from one to another and asked:

"Who is this stranger?"

"Why, it's Button-Bright, of course," answered

Trot. "If anyone ever finds a lost boy, he can make up his mind it's Button-Bright. But how he ever came to be lost in this far-away country is more'n I can make out."

"Where does he belong?" inquired the Ork.

"His home used to be in Philadelphia, I think; but I'm quite sure Button-Bright doesn't belong anywhere."

"That's right," said the boy, nodding his head as he swallowed the second mouthful.

"Everyone belongs somewhere," remarked the Ork.

"Not me," insisted Button-Bright. "I'm half way 'round the world from Philadelphia, and I've lost my Magic Umbrella, that used to carry me anywhere. Stands to reason that if I can't get back I haven't any home. But I don't care much. This is a pretty good country, Trot. I've had lots of fun here."

By this time the Mountain Ear had secured the boy's cap and was listening to the conversation with much interest.

"It seems you know this poor, snow-covered castaway," he said.

"Yes, indeed," answered Trot. "We made a journey together to Sky Island, once, and were good friends."

"Well, then I'm glad I saved his life," said the Bumpy Man.

"Much obliged, Mr. Knobs," said Button-Bright, sitting up and staring at him, "but I don't believe you've saved anything except some popcorn that I might have eaten had you not disturbed me. It was nice and warm in that bank of popcorn, and there was plenty to eat. What made you dig me out? And what makes you so bumpy everywhere?"

"As for the bumps," replied the man, looking at himself with much pride, "I was born with them and

I suspect they were a gift from the fairies. They make me look rugged and big, like the mountain I serve."

"All right," said Button-Bright and began eating popcorn again.

It had stopped snowing, now, and great flocks of birds were gathering around the mountain-side, eating the popcorn with much eagerness and scarcely noticing the people at all. There were birds of every size and color, most of them having gorgeous feathers and plumes.

"Just look at them!" exclaimed the Ork scornfully. "Aren't they dreadful creatures, all covered with feathers?"

"I think they're beautiful," said Trot, and this made the Ork so indignant that he went back into the house and sulked.

Button-Bright reached out his hand and caught a big bird by the leg. At once it rose into the air and it was so strong that it nearly carried the little boy with it. He let go the leg in a hurry and the bird flew down again and began to eat of the popcorn, not being frightened in the least.

This gave Cap'n Bill an idea. He felt in his pocket and drew out several pieces of stout string. Moving very quietly, so as to not alarm the birds, he crept up to several of the biggest ones and tied cords around their legs, thus making them prisoners. The birds were so intent on their eating that they did not notice what had happened to them, and when about twenty had been captured in this manner Cap'n Bill tied the ends of all the strings together and fastened them to a huge stone, so they could not escape.

The Bumpy Man watched the old sailor's actions with much curiosity.

"The birds will be quiet until they've eaten up all the snow," he said, "but then they will want to fly away to their homes. Tell me, sir, what will the poor things do when they find they can't fly?"

"It may worry 'em a little," replied Cap'n Bill, "but they're not going to be hurt if they take it easy and behave themselves."

Our friends had all made a good breakfast of the delicious popcorn and now they walked toward the house again. Button-Bright walked beside Trot and held her hand in his, because they were old friends and he liked the little girl very much. The boy was not so old as Trot, and small as she was he was half a head shorter in height. The most remarkable thing about Button-Bright was that he was always quiet and composed, whatever happened, and nothing was ever able to astonish him. Trot liked him because he was not rude and never tried to plague her. Cap'n Bill liked him because he had found the boy cheerful and brave at all times, and willing to do anything he was asked to do.

When they came to the house Trot sniffed the air and asked: "Don't I smell perfume?"

"I think you do," said the Bumpy Man. "You smell violets, and that proves there is a breeze spring- ing up from the south. All our winds and breezes are

perfumed and for that reason we are glad to have them blow in our direction. The south breeze always has a violet odor; the north breeze has the fragrance of wild roses; the east breeze is perfumed with lilies-of-the-valley and the west wind with lilac blossoms. So we need no weathervane to tell us which way the wind is blowing. We have only to smell the perfume and it informs us at once."

Inside the house they found the Ork, and Button-Bright regarded the strange, bird-like creature with curious interest. After examining it closely for a time he asked:

"Which way does your tail whirl?"

"Either way," said the Ork.

Button-Bright put out his hand and tried to spin it.

"Don't do that!" exclaimed the Ork.

"Why not?" inquired the boy.

"Because it happens to be my tail, and I reserve the right to whirl it myself," explained the Ork.

"Let's go out and fly somewhere," proposed Button-Bright. "I want to see how the tail works."

"Not now," said the Ork. "I appreciate your interest in me, which I fully deserve; but I only fly when I am going somewhere, and if I got started I might not stop."

"That reminds me," remarked Cap'n Bill, "to ask you, friend Ork, how we are going to get away from here?"

"Get away!" exclaimed the Bumpy Man. "Why don't you stay here? You won't find any nicer place than Mo."

"Have you been anywhere else, sir?"

"No; I can't say that I have," admitted the Mountain Ear.

"Then permit me to say you're no judge," declared Cap'n Bill. "But you haven't answered my question, friend Ork. How are we to get away from this mountain?"

The Ork reflected a while before he answered.

"I might carry one of you — the boy or the girl — upon my back," said he, "but three big people are more than I can manage, although I have carried two of you for a short distance. You ought not to have eaten those purple berries so soon."

"P'r'aps we did make a mistake," Cap'n Bill acknowledged.

"Or we might have brought some of those lavender berries with us, instead of so many purple ones," suggested Trot regretfully.

Cap'n Bill made no reply to this statement, which

showed he did not fully agree with the little girl; but he fell into deep thought, with wrinkled brows, and finally he said:

"If those purple berries would make anything grow bigger, whether it'd eaten the lavender ones or not, I could find a way out of our troubles."

They did not understand this speech and looked at the old sailor as if expecting him to explain what he meant. But just then a chorus of shrill cries rose from outside.

"Here! Let me go — let me go!" the voices seemed to say. "Why are we insulted in this way? Mountain Ear, come and help us!"

Trot ran to the window and looked out.

"It's the birds you caught, Cap'n," she said. "I didn't know they could talk."

"Oh, yes; all the birds in Mo are educated to talk," said the Bumpy Man. Then he looked at Cap'n Bill uneasily and added: "Won't you let the poor things go?"

"I'll see," replied the sailor, and walked out to where the birds were fluttering and complaining because the strings would not allow them to fly away.

"Listen to me!" he cried, and at once they became still. "We three people who are strangers in your land want to go to some other country, and we want three of you birds to carry us there. We know we are asking a great favor, but it's the only way we can think of — excep' walkin', an' I'm not much good at that because I've a wooden leg. Besides, Trot an'

Button-Bright are too small to undertake a long and tiresome journey. Now, tell me: Which three of you birds will consent to carry us?"

The birds looked at one another as if greatly astonished. Then one of them replied:

"You must be crazy, old man. Not one of us is big

enough to fly with even the smallest of your party."

"I'll fix the matter of size," promised Cap'n Bill. "If three of you will agree to carry us, I'll make you big an' strong enough to do it, so it won't worry you a bit."

The birds considered this gravely. Living in a magic country, they had no doubt but that the strange one-legged man could do what he said. After a little, one of them asked:

"If you make us big, would we stay big always?"

"I think so," replied Cap'n Bill.

They chattered a while among themselves and then the bird that had first spoken said: "I'll go, for one."

"So will I," said another; and after a pause a third said: "I'll go, too."

Perhaps more would have volunteered, for it seemed that for some reason they all longed to be bigger than they were; but three were enough for Cap'n Bill's purpose and so he promptly released all the others, who immediately flew away.

The three that remained were cousins, and all were of the same brilliant plumage and in size about as large as eagles. When Trot questioned them she found they were quite young, having only abandoned their nests a few weeks before. They were strong young birds, with clear, brave eyes, and the little girl decided they were the most beautiful of all the feathered creatures she had ever seen.

Cap'n Bill now took from his pocket the wooden box with the sliding cover and removed the three purple berries, which were still in good condition.

"Eat these," he said, and gave one to each of the birds. They obeyed, finding the fruit very pleasant to taste. In a few seconds they began to grow in size and grew so fast that Trot feared they would never stop. But they finally did stop growing, and then they were much larger than the Ork, and nearly the size of full-grown ostriches.

Cap'n Bill was much pleased by this result.

"You can carry us now, all right," said he.

The birds strutted around with pride, highly pleased with their immense size.

"I don't see, though," said Trot doubtfully, "how we're going to ride on their backs without falling off."

"We're not going to ride on their backs," answered Cap'n Bill. "I'm going to make swings for us to ride in."

He then asked the Bumpy Man for some rope, but the man had no rope. He had, however, an old suit of gray clothes which he gladly presented to Cap'n Bill, who cut the cloth into strips and twisted it so that it was almost as strong as rope. With this material he attached to each bird a swing that dangled below its feet, and Button-Bright made a trial flight in one of them to prove that it was safe and comfortable. When all this had been arranged one of the birds asked:

"Where do you wish us to take you?"

"Why, just follow the Ork," said Cap'n Bill. "He will be our leader, and wherever the Ork flies you are

to fly, and wherever the Ork lands you are to land. Is that satisfactory?"

The birds declared it was quite satisfactory, so Cap'n Bill took counsel with the Ork.

"On our way here," said that peculiar creature, "I noticed a broad, sandy desert at the left of me, on which was no living thing."

"Then we'd better keep away from it," replied the sailor.

"Not so," insisted the Ork. "I have found, on my

travels, that the most pleasant countries often lie in the midst of deserts; so I think it would be wise for us to fly over this desert and discover what lies beyond it. For in the direction we came from lies the ocean, as we well know, and beyond here is this strange Land of Mo, which we do not care to explore. On one side, as we can see from this mountain, is a broad expanse of plain, and on the other the desert. For my part, I vote for the desert."

"What do you say, Trot?" inquired Cap'n Bill.

"It's all the same to me," she replied.

No one thought of asking Button-Bright's opinion, so it was decided to fly over the desert. They bade good-bye to the Bumpy Man and thanked him for his kindness and hospitality. Then they seated themselves in the swings — one for each bird — and told the Ork to start away and they would follow.

The whirl of the Ork's tail astonished the birds at first, but after he had gone a short distance they rose in the air, carrying their passengers easily, and flew with strong, regular strokes of their great wings in the wake of their leader.

## CHAPTER 9

# The Kingdom of Jinxland

Trot rode with more comfort than she had expected, although the swing swayed so much that she had to hold on tight with both hands. Cap'n Bill's bird followed the Ork, and Trot came next, with Button-Bright trailing behind her. It was quite an imposing procession, but unfortunately there was no one to see it, for the Ork had headed straight for the great sandy desert and in a few minutes after starting they were flying high over the broad waste, where no living thing could exist.

The little girl thought this would be a bad place for the birds to lose strength, or for the cloth ropes to give way; but although she could not help feeling a trifle nervous and fidgety she had confidence in the huge and brilliantly plumaged bird that bore her, as well as in Cap'n Bill's knowledge of how to twist and fasten a rope so it would hold.

That was a remarkably big desert. There was nothing to relieve the monotony of view and every minute seemed an hour and every hour a day. Disagreeable fumes and gases rose from the sands, which would have been deadly to the travelers had they not been so high in the air. As it was, Trot was beginning to feel sick, when a breath of fresher air filled her nostrils and on looking ahead she saw a great cloud of pink-tinted mist. Even while she wondered what it could be, the Ork plunged boldly into the mist and the other birds followed. She could see nothing for a time, nor could the bird which carried her see where the Ork had gone, but it kept flying as sturdily as ever and in a few moments the mist was passed and the girl saw a most beautiful landscape spread out below her, extending as far as her eye could reach.

She saw bits of forest, verdure clothed hills, fields of waving grain, fountains, rivers and lakes; and throughout the scene were scattered groups of pretty houses and a few grand castles and palaces.

Over all this delightful landscape — which from Trot's high perch seemed like a magnificent painted picture — was a rosy glow such as we sometimes see in the west at sunset. In this case, however, it was not in the west only, but everywhere.

No wonder the Ork paused to circle slowly over this lovely country. The other birds followed his action, all eyeing the place with equal delight. Then, as with one accord, the four formed a group and slowly sailed downward. This brought them to that part of the newly-discovered land which bordered on the desert's edge; but it was just as pretty here as anywhere, so the Ork and the birds alighted and the three passengers at once got out of their swings.

"Oh, Cap'n Bill, isn't this fine an' dandy?" exclaimed Trot rapturously. "How lucky we were to discover this beautiful country!"

"The country seems rather high class, I'll admit, Trot," replied the old sailor-man, looking around him, "but we don't know, as yet, what its people are like."

"No one could live in such a country without being happy and good — I'm sure of that," she said earnestly. "Don't you think so, Button-Bright?"

"I'm not thinking, just now," answered the little boy. "It tires me to think, and I never seem to gain anything by it. When we see the people who live here we will know what they are like, and no 'mount of thinking will make them any different."

"That's true enough," said the Ork. "But now I want to make a proposal. While you are getting acquainted with this new country, which looks as if it contains everything to make one happy, I would like to fly along — all by myself — and see if I can find my home on the other side of the great desert. If I do, I will stay there, of course. But if I fail to find Orkland I will return to you in a week, to see if I can do anything more to assist you."

They were sorry to lose their queer companion, but could offer no objection to the plan; so the Ork bade them good-bye and rising swiftly in the air, he flew over the country and was soon lost to view in the distance.

The three birds which had carried our friends now begged permission to return by the way they had come, to their own homes, saying they were anxious to show their families how big they had become. So Cap'n Bill and Trot and Button-Bright all thanked them gratefully for their assistance and soon the birds began their long flight toward the Land of Mo.

Being now left to themselves in this strange land,

the three comrades selected a pretty pathway and began walking along it. They believed this path would lead them to a splendid castle which they espied in the distance, the turrets of which towered far above the tops of the trees which surrounded it. It did not seem very far away, so they sauntered on slowly, admiring the beautiful ferns and flowers that lined the pathway and listening to the singing of the birds and the soft chirping of the grasshoppers.

Presently the path wound over a little hill. In a valley that lay beyond the hill was a tiny cottage surrounded by flower beds and fruit trees. On the shady porch of the cottage they saw, as they approached, a pleasant faced woman sitting amidst a group of children, to whom she was telling stories. The children quickly discovered the strangers and ran toward them with exclamations of astonishment, so that Trot and her friends became the center of a curious group, all chattering excitedly. Cap'n Bill's wooden leg seemed to arouse the wonder of the children, as they could not understand why he had not two meat legs. This attention seemed to please the old sailor, who patted the heads of the children kindly and then, raising his hat to the woman, he inquired:

"Can you tell us, madam, just what country this is?"

She stared hard at all three of the strangers as she replied briefly: "Jinxland."

"Oh!" exclaimed Cap'n Bill, with a puzzled look. "And where is Jinxland, please?"

"In the Quadling Country," said she.

"What!" cried Trot, in sudden excitement. "Do you mean to say this is the Quadling Country of the Land of Oz?"

"To be sure I do," the woman answered. "Every bit of land that is surrounded by the great desert is the Land of Oz, as you ought to know as well as I do; but I'm sorry to say that Jinxland is separated from the rest of the Quadling Country by that row of high mountains you see yonder, which have such steep sides that no one can cross them. So we live here all by ourselves, and are ruled by our own King, instead of by Ozma of Oz."

"I've been to the Land of Oz before," said Button-Bright, "but I've never been here."

"Did you ever hear of Jinxland before?" asked Trot.

"No," said Button-Bright.

"It is on the Map of Oz, though," asserted the woman, "and it's a fine country, I assure you. If only," she added, and then paused to look around her with a frightened expression. "If only —" here she stopped again, as if not daring to go on with her speech.

"If only what, ma'am?" asked Cap'n Bill.

The woman sent the children into the house. Then she came closer to the strangers and whispered: "If only we had a different King, we would be very happy and contented."

"What's the matter with your King?" asked Trot, curiously. But the woman seemed frightened to have said so much. She retreated to her porch, merely saying:

"The King punishes severely any treason on the part of his subjects."

"What's treason?" asked Button-Bright.

"In this case," replied Cap'n Bill, "treason seems to consist of knockin' the King; but I guess we know his disposition now as well as if the lady had said more."

"I wonder," said Trot, going up to the woman, "if you could spare us something to eat. We haven't had anything but popcorn and lemonade for a long time."

"Bless your heart! Of course I can spare you some food," the woman answered, and entering her cottage she soon returned with a tray loaded with sandwiches, cakes and cheese. One of the children drew a bucket of clear, cold water from a spring and the three wanderers ate heartily and enjoyed the good things immensely.

When Button-Bright could eat no more he filled the pockets of his jacket with cakes and cheese, and not even the children objected to this. Indeed they all seemed pleased to see the strangers eat, so Cap'n Bill decided that no matter what the King of Jinxland was like, the people would prove friendly and hospitable.

"Whose castle is that, yonder, ma'am?" he asked,

waving his hand toward the towers that rose above the trees.

"It belongs to his Majesty, King Krewl." she said.

"Oh, indeed; and does he live there?"

"When he is not out hunting with his fierce courtiers and war captains," she replied.

# The Scarecrow of Oz

"Is he hunting now?" Trot inquired.

"I do not know, my dear. The less we know about the King's actions the safer we are."

It was evident the woman did not like to talk about King Krewl and so, having finished their meal, they said good-bye and continued along the pathway.

"Don't you think we'd better keep away from that King's castle, Cap'n?" asked Trot.

"Well," said he, "King Krewl would find out, sooner or later, that we are in his country, so we may as well face the music now. Perhaps he isn't quite so bad as that woman thinks he is. Kings aren't always popular with their people, you know, even if they do the best they know how."

"Ozma is pop'lar," said Button-Bright.

"Ozma is diff'rent from any other Ruler, from all I've heard," remarked Trot musingly, as she walked beside the boy. "And, after all, we are really in the Land of Oz, where Ozma rules ev'ry King and ev'rybody else. I never heard of anybody getting hurt in her dominions, did you, Button-Bright?"

"Not when she knows about it," he replied. "But those birds landed us in just the wrong place, seems to me. They might have carried us right on, over that row of mountains, to the Em'rald City."

# Chapter Nine

"True enough," said Cap'n Bill; "but they didn't, an' so we must make the best of Jinxland. Let's try not to be afraid."

"Oh, I'm not very scared," said Button-Bright, pausing to look at a pink rabbit that popped its head out of a hole in the field near by.

"Nor am I," added Trot. "Really, Cap'n, I'm so glad to be anywhere at all in the wonderful fairyland of Oz that I think I'm the luckiest girl in all the world. Dorothy lives in the Em'rald City, you know, and so does the Scarecrow and the Tin Woodman and Tik-Tok and the Shaggy Man — and all the rest of 'em that we've heard so much about — not to mention Ozma, who must be the sweetest and loveliest girl in all the world!"

"Take your time, Trot," advised Button-Bright. "You don't have to say it all in one breath, you know. And you haven't mentioned half of the curious people in the Em'rald City."

"That 'ere Em'rald City," said Cap'n Bill impressively, "happens to be on the other side o' those mountains, that we're told no one is able to cross. I don't want to discourage of you, Trot, but we're a'most as much separated from your Ozma an' Dorothy as we were when we lived in Californy."

# The Scarecrow of Oz

There was so much truth in this statement that they all walked on in silence for some time. Finally they reached the grove of stately trees that bordered the grounds of the King's castle. They had gone halfway through it when the sound of sobbing, as of someone in bitter distress, reached their ears and caused them to halt abruptly.

## CHAPTER 10

# Pon, the Gardener's Boy

It was Button-Bright who first discovered, lying on his face beneath a broad spreading tree near the pathway, a young man whose body shook with the force of his sobs. He was dressed in a long brown smock and had sandals on his feet, betokening one in humble life. His head was bare and showed a shock of brown, curly hair. Button-Bright looked down on the young man and said:

"Who cares, anyhow?"

"I do!" cried the young man, interrupting his sobs to roll over, face upward, that he might see who had spoken. "I care, for my heart is broken!"

"Can't you get another one?" asked the little boy.

"I don't want another!" wailed the young man.

By this time Trot and Cap'n Bill arrived at the spot and the girl leaned over and said in a sympathetic voice:

"Tell us your troubles and perhaps we may help you."

The youth sat up, then, and bowed politely. Afterward he got upon his feet, but still kept wringing his hands as he tried to choke down his sobs. Trot thought he was very brave to control such awful agony so well.

"My name is Pon," he began. "I'm the gardener's boy."

"Then the gardener of the King is your father, I suppose," said Trot.

"Not my father, but my master," was the reply. "I do the work and the gardener gives the orders. And it was not my fault, in the least, that the Princess Gloria fell in love with me."

"Did she, really?" asked the little girl.

"I don't see why," remarked Button-Bright, staring at the youth.

"And who may the Princess Gloria be?" inquired Cap'n Bill.

"She is the niece of King Krewl, who is her guardian. The Princess lives in the castle and is the loveliest and sweetest maiden in all Jinxland. She is fond of flowers and used to walk in the gardens with her attendants. At such times, if I was working at my tasks, I used to cast down my eyes as Gloria passed me; but one day I glanced up and found her gazing at me with a very tender look in her eyes. The next day she dismissed her attendants and, coming to my side, began to talk with me. She said I had touched her heart as no other young man had ever done. I kissed her hand. Just then the King came around a bend in the walk. He struck me with his fist and kicked me with his foot. Then he seized the arm of the Princess and rudely dragged her into the castle."

"Wasn't he awful!" gasped Trot indignantly.

"He is a very abrupt King," said Pon, "so it was the least I could expect. Up to that time I had not thought of loving Princess Gloria, but realizing it would be impolite not to return her love, I did so. We met at evening, now and then, and she told me the King wanted her to marry a rich courtier named Googly-Goo, who is old enough to be Gloria's father. She has refused Googly-Goo thirty-nine times, but he still persists and has brought many rich presents to bribe the King. On that account King Krewl has commanded his niece to marry the old man, but the Princess has assured me, time and again, that she will wed only me. This morning we happened to meet in the grape arbor and as I was respectfully saluting the cheek of the Princess, two of the King's guards seized me and beat me terribly before the very eyes of Gloria, whom the King himself held back so she could not interfere."

"Why, this King must be a monster!" cried Trot.

"He is far worse than that," said Pon, mournfully.

"But, see here," interrupted Cap'n Bill, who had listened carefully to Pon. "This King may not be so much to blame, after all. Kings are proud folks, because they're so high an' mighty, an' it isn't reasonable for a royal Princess to marry a common gardener's boy."

"It isn't right," declared Button-Bright. "A Princess should marry a Prince."

"I'm not a common gardener's boy," protested Pon. "If I had my rights I would be the King instead of Krewl. As it is, I'm a Prince, and as royal as any man in Jinxland."

"How does that come?" asked Cap'n Bill.

"My father used to be the King and Krewl was his Prime Minister. But one day while out hunting, King Phearse — that was my father's name — had a quarrel with Krewl and tapped him gently on the nose with the knuckles of his closed hand. This so provoked the wicked Krewl that he tripped my father backward, so that he fell into a deep pond. At once Krewl threw in a mass of heavy stones, which so weighted down my poor father that his body could not rise again to the surface. It is impossible to kill anyone in this land, as perhaps you know, but when my father was pressed down into the mud at the bottom of the deep pool and the stones held him so he could never escape, he was of no more use to himself or the world than if he had died. Knowing this, Krewl proclaimed himself King, taking possession of the royal castle and driving all my father's people out. I was a small boy, then, but when I grew up I became a gardener. I have served King Krewl without his knowing that I am the son of the same King Phearse whom he so cruelly made away with."

"My, but that's a terr'bly exciting story!" said Trot, drawing a long breath. "But tell us, Pon, who was Gloria's father?"

"Oh, he was the King before my father," replied

Pon. "Father was Prime Minister for King Kynd, who was Gloria's father. She was only a baby when King Kynd fell into the Great Gulf that lies just this side of the mountains — the same mountains that separate Jinxland from the rest of the Land of Oz. It is said the Great Gulf has no bottom; but, however that may be, King Kynd has never been seen again and my father became King in his place."

"Seems to me," said Trot, "that if Gloria had her rights she would be Queen of Jinxland."

"Well, her father was a King," admitted Pon, "and so was my father; so we are of equal rank, although she's a great lady and I'm a humble gardener's boy. I can't see why we should not marry if we want to — except that King Krewl won't let us."

"It's a sort of mixed-up mess, taken altogether," remarked Cap'n Bill. "But we are on our way to visit King Krewl, and if we get a chance, young man, we'll put in a good word for you."

"Do, please!" begged Pon.

"Was it the flogging you got that broke your heart?" inquired Button-Bright.

"Why, it helped to break it, of course," said Pon.

"I'd get it fixed up, if I were you," advised the boy, tossing a pebble at a chipmunk in a tree.

"You ought to give Gloria just as good a heart as she gives you."

"That's common sense," agreed Cap'n Bill. So they left the gardener's boy standing beside the path, and resumed their journey toward the castle.

## CHAPTER 11

# The Wicked King and Googly-Goo

When our friends approached the great doorway of the castle they found it guarded by several soldiers dressed in splendid uniforms. They were armed with swords and lances. Cap'n Bill walked straight up to them and asked:

"Does the King happen to be at home?"

"His Magnificent and Glorious Majesty, King Krewl, is at present inhabiting his Royal Castle," was the stiff reply.

"Then I guess we'll go in an' say how-d'ye-do," continued Cap'n Bill, attempting to enter the doorway. But a soldier barred his way with a lance.

# Chapter Eleven

"Who are you, what are your names, and where do you come from?" demanded the soldier.

"You wouldn't know if we told you," returned the sailor, "seein' as we're strangers in a strange land."

"Oh, if you are strangers you will be permitted to enter," said the soldier, lowering his lance. "His Majesty is very fond of strangers."

"Do many strangers come here?" asked Trot.

"You are the first that ever came to our country," said the man. "But his Majesty has often said that if strangers ever arrived in Jinxland he would see that they had a very exciting time."

Cap'n Bill scratched his chin thoughtfully. He wasn't very favorably impressed by this last remark. But he decided that as there was no way of escape from Jinxland it would be wise to confront the King boldly and try to win his favor. So they entered the castle, escorted by one of the soldiers.

It was certainly a fine castle, with many large rooms, all beautifully furnished. The passages were winding and handsomely decorated, and after following several of these the soldier led them into an open court that occupied the very center of the huge building. It was surrounded on every side by high turreted walls, and contained beds of flowers, fountains and walks of many colored marbles which were matched together in quaint designs. In an open space near the middle of the court they saw a group of courtiers and their ladies, who surrounded a lean man who wore upon his head a jeweled crown. His face was hard and sullen and through the slits of his half-closed eyelids the eyes glowed like coals of fire. He was dressed in brilliant satins and velvets and was seated in a golden throne-chair.

This personage was King Krewl, and as soon as Cap'n Bill saw him the old sailor knew at once that he was not going to like the King of Jinxland.

"Hello! who's here?" said his Majesty, with a deep scowl.

"Strangers, Sire," answered the soldier, bowing so low that his forehead touched the marble tiles.

"Strangers, eh? Well, well; what an unexpected visit! Advance, strangers, and give an account of yourselves."

The King's voice was as harsh as his features. Trot shuddered a little but Cap'n Bill calmly replied:

"There ain't much for us to say, 'cept as we've arrived to look over your country an' see how we like it. Judgin' from the way you speak, you don't know who we are, or you'd be jumpin' up to shake hands an' offer us seats. Kings usually treat us pretty well, in the great big Outside World where we come from, but in this little kingdom — which don't amount to much, anyhow — folks don't seem to 'a' got much culchure."

The King listened with amazement to this bold speech, first with a frown and then gazing at the two children and the old sailor with evident curiosity. The courtiers were dumb with fear, for no one had ever dared speak in such a manner to their self-willed, cruel King before. His Majesty, however, was somewhat frightened, for cruel people are always cowards, and he feared these mysterious strangers might possess magic powers that would destroy him unless he treated them well. So he commanded his people to give the new arrivals seats, and they obeyed with trembling haste.

After being seated, Cap'n Bill lighted his pipe and began puffing smoke from it, a sight so strange to them that it filled them all with wonder. Presently the King asked:

"How did you penetrate to this hidden country? Did you cross the desert or the mountains?"

"Desert," answered Cap'n Bill, as if the task were too easy to be worth talking about.

"Indeed! No one has ever been able to do that before," said the King.

"Well, it's easy enough, if you know how," asserted Cap'n Bill, so carelessly that it greatly impressed his hearers. The King shifted in his throne uneasily. He was more afraid of these strangers than before.

"Do you intend to stay long in Jinxland?" was his next anxious question.

"Depends on how we like it," said Cap'n Bill. "Just now I might suggest to your Majesty to order some rooms got ready for us in your dinky little castle here. And a royal banquet, with some fried onions an' pickled tripe, would set easy on our stomicks an' make us a bit happier than we are now."

"Your wishes shall be attended to," said King Krewl, but his eyes flashed from between their slits in a wicked way that made Trot hope the food wouldn't be poisoned. At the King's command several of his attendants hastened away to give the proper orders to the castle servants and no sooner were they gone than a skinny old man entered the courtyard and bowed before the King.

This disagreeable person was dressed in rich velvets, with many furbelows and laces. He was covered with golden chains, finely wrought rings and jeweled orna-

ments. He walked with mincing steps and glared at all the courtiers as if he considered himself far superior to any or all of them.

"Well, well, your Majesty; what news — what news?" he demanded, in a shrill, cracked voice.

The King gave him a surly look.

"No news, Lord Googly-Goo, except that strangers have arrived," he said.

Googly-Goo cast a contemptuous glance at Cap'n Bill and a disdainful one at Trot and Button-Bright. Then he said:

"Strangers do not interest me, your Majesty. But the Princess Gloria is very interesting — very interesting, indeed! What does she say, Sire? Will she marry me?"

"Ask her," retorted the King.

"I have, many times; and every time she has refused."

"Well?" said the King harshly.

"Well," said Googly-Goo in a jaunty tone, "a bird that *can* sing, and *won't* sing, must be *made* to sing."

"Huh!" sneered the King. "That's easy, with a bird; but a girl is harder to manage."

"Still," persisted Googly-Goo, "we must overcome difficulties. The chief trouble is that Gloria fancies she loves that miserable gardener's boy, Pon. Suppose we throw Pon into the Great Gulf, your Majesty?"

"It would do you no good," returned the King. "She would still love him."

"Too bad, too bad!" sighed Googly-Goo. "I have laid aside more than a bushel of precious gems — each worth a king's ransom — to present to your Majesty on the day I wed Gloria."

The King's eyes sparkled, for he loved wealth above everything; but the next moment he frowned deeply again.

"It won't help us to kill Pon," he muttered. "What we must do is kill Gloria's love for Pon."

"That is better, if you can find a way to do it," agreed Googly-Goo. "Everything would come right if you could kill Gloria's love for that gardener's boy. Really, Sire, now that I come to think of it, there must be fully a bushel and a half of those jewels!"

Just then a messenger entered the court to say that the banquet was prepared for the strangers. So Cap'n Bill, Trot and Button-Bright entered the castle and were taken to a room where a fine feast was spread upon the table.

"I don't like that Lord Googly-Goo," remarked Trot as she was busily eating.

"Nor I," said Cap'n Bill. "But from the talk we heard I guess the gardener's boy won't get the Princess."

"Perhaps not," returned the girl; "but I hope old Googly doesn't get her, either."

"The King means to sell her for all those jewels," observed Button-Bright, his mouth half full of cake and jam.

"Poor Princess!" sighed Trot. "I'm sorry for her, although I've never seen her. But if she says no to Googly-Goo, and means it, what can they do?"

"Don't let us worry about a strange Princess," advised Cap'n Bill. "I've a notion we're not too safe, ourselves, with this cruel King."

The two children felt the same way and all three were rather solemn during the remainder of the meal.

When they had eaten, the servants escorted them to their rooms. Cap'n Bill's room was way to one end of the castle, very high up, and Trot's room was at the opposite end, rather low down. As for Button-Bright, they placed him in the middle, so that all were as far apart as they could possibly be. They didn't like this arrangement very well, but all the rooms were handsomely furnished and being guests of the King they dared not complain.

After the strangers had left the courtyard the King and Googly-Goo had a long talk together, and the King said:

"I cannot force Gloria to marry you just now, because those strangers may interfere. I suspect that the wooden-legged man possesses great magical powers, or he would never have been able to carry himself and those children across the deadly desert."

"I don't like him; he looks dangerous," answered

Googly-Goo. "But perhaps you are mistaken about his being a wizard. Why don't you test his powers?"

"How?" asked the King.

"Send for the Wicked Witch. She will tell you in a moment whether that wooden-legged person is a common man or a magician."

"Ha! that's a good idea," cried the King. "Why didn't I think of the Wicked Witch before? But the woman demands rich rewards for her services."

"Never mind; I will pay her," promised the wealthy Googly-Goo.

So a servant was dispatched to summon the Wicked Witch, who lived but a few leagues from King Krewl's castle. While they awaited her, the withered old courtier proposed that they pay a visit to Princess Gloria and see if she was not now in a more complaisant mood. So the two started away together and searched the castle over without finding Gloria.

At last Googly-Goo suggested she might be in the rear garden, which was a large park filled with bushes and trees and surrounded by a high wall. And what was their anger, when they turned a corner of the path, to find in a quiet nook the beautiful Princess, and kneeling before her, Pon, the gardener's boy!

With a roar of rage the King dashed forward; but

Pon had scaled the wall by means of a ladder, which still stood in its place, and when he saw the King coming he ran up the ladder and made good his escape. But this left Gloria confronted by her angry guardian, the King, and by old Googly-Goo, who was trembling with a fury he could not express in words.

Seizing the Princess by her arm the King dragged her back to the castle. Pushing her into a room on the lower floor he locked the door upon the unhappy girl. And at that moment the arrival of the Wicked Witch was announced.

Hearing this, the King smiled, as a tiger smiles, showing his teeth. And Googly-Goo smiled, as a serpent smiles, for he had no teeth except a couple of fangs. And having frightened each other with these smiles the two dreadful men went away to the Royal Council Chamber to meet the Wicked Witch.

Queen Gloria

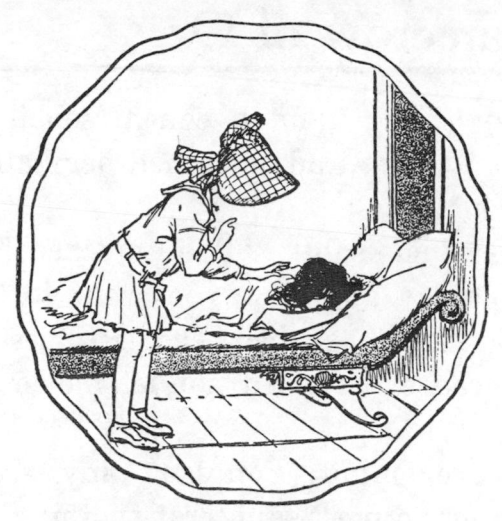

## CHAPTER 12

# The Wooden-Legged Grass-Hopper

Now it so happened that Trot, from the window of her room, had witnessed the meeting of the lovers in the garden and had seen the King come and drag Gloria away. The little girl's heart went out in sympathy for the poor Princess, who seemed to her to be one of the sweetest and loveliest young ladies she had ever seen, so she crept along the passages and from a hidden niche saw Gloria locked in her room.

The key was still in the lock, so when the King had gone away, followed by Googly-Goo, Trot stole up to the door, turned the key and entered. The

Princess lay prone upon a couch, sobbing bitterly. Trot went up to her and smoothed her hair and tried to comfort her.

"Don't cry," she said. "I've unlocked the door, so you can go away any time you want to."

"It isn't that," sobbed the Princess. "I am unhappy because they will not let me love Pon, the gardener's boy!"

"Well, never mind; Pon isn't any great shakes, anyhow, seems to me," said Trot soothingly. "There are lots of other people you can love."

Gloria rolled over on the couch and looked at the little girl reproachfully.

"Pon has won my heart, and I can't help loving him," she explained. Then with sudden indignation she added: "But I'll never love Googly-Goo — never, as long as I live!"

"I should say not!" replied Trot. "Pon may not be much good, but old Googly is very, very bad. Hunt around, and I'm sure you'll find someone worth your love. You're very pretty, you know, and almost anyone ought to love you."

"You don't understand, my dear," said Gloria, as she wiped the tears from her eyes with a dainty lace handkerchief bordered with pearls. "When you are older you will realize that a young lady cannot decide whom she will love, or choose the most worthy. Her heart alone decides for her, and whomsoever her heart selects, she must love, whether he amounts to much or not."

Trot was a little puzzled by this speech, which seemed to her unreasonable; but she made no reply and presently Gloria's grief softened and she began to question the little girl about herself and her adventures. Trot told her how they had happened to come to Jinxland, and all about Cap'n Bill and the Ork and Pessim and the Bumpy Man.

While they were thus conversing together, getting more and more friendly as they became better acquainted, in the Council Chamber the King and Googly-Goo were talking with the Wicked Witch.

This evil creature was old and ugly. She had lost one eye and wore a black patch over it, so the people of Jinxland had named her "Blinkie." Of course witches are forbidden to exist in the Land of Oz, but Jinxland was so far removed from the center of Ozma's dominions, and so absolutely cut off from it by the steep mountains and the bottomless gulf, that the laws of Oz were not obeyed very well in that country. So there were several witches in Jinxland who were the terror of the people, but King Krewl favored them and permitted them to exercise their evil sorcery.

Blinkie was the leader of all the other witches and therefore the most hated and feared. The King used her witchcraft at times to assist him in carrying out his cruelties and revenge, but he was always obliged to pay Blinkie large sums of money or heaps of precious jewels before she would undertake an enchantment. This made him hate the old woman almost as much as his subjects did, but to-day Lord Googly-Goo had agreed to pay the witch's price, so the King greeted her with gracious favor.

"Can you destroy the love of Princess Gloria for the gardener's boy?" inquired his Majesty.

The Wicked Witch thought about it before she replied:

"That's a hard question to answer. I can do lots of clever magic, but love is a stubborn thing to conquer. When you think you've killed it, it's liable to bob up again as strong as ever. I believe love and cats have nine lives. In other words, killing love is a hard job, even for a skillful witch, but I believe I can do something that will answer your purpose just as well."

"What is that?" asked the King.

"I can freeze the girl's heart. I've got a special incantation for that, and when Gloria's heart is thoroughly frozen she can no longer love Pon."

"Just the thing!" exclaimed Googly-Goo, and the King was likewise much pleased.

They bargained a long time as to the price, but finally the old courtier agreed to pay the Wicked Witch's demands. It was arranged that they should take Gloria to Blinkie's house the next day, to have her heart frozen.

Then King Krewl mentioned to the old hag the strangers who had that day arrived in Jinxland, and said to her:

"I think the two children — the boy and the girl — are unable to harm me, but I have a suspicion that the wooden-legged man is a powerful wizard."

The witch's face wore a troubled look when she heard this.

"If you are right," she said, "this wizard might spoil my incantation and interfere with me in other ways. So it will be best for me to meet this stranger at once and match my magic against his, to decide which is the stronger."

"All right," said the King. "Come with me and I will lead you to the man's room."

# Chapter Twelve

Googly-Goo did not accompany them, as he was obliged to go home to get the money and jewels he had promised to pay old Blinkie, so the other two climbed several flights of stairs and went through many passages until they came to the room occupied by Cap'n Bill.

The sailor-man, finding his bed soft and inviting, and being tired with the adventures he had experienced, had decided to take a nap. When the Wicked Witch and the King softly opened his door and entered, Cap'n Bill was snoring with such vigor that he did not hear them at all.

Blinkie approached the bed and with her one eye anxiously stared at the sleeping stranger.

"Ah," she said in a soft whisper, "I believe you are right, King Krewl. The man looks to me like a very powerful wizard. But by good luck I have caught him asleep, so I shall transform him before he wakes up, giving him such a form that he will be unable to oppose me."

"Careful!" cautioned the King, also speaking low. "If he discovers what you are doing he may destroy you, and that would annoy me because I need you to attend to Gloria."

But the Wicked Witch realized as well as he did

that she must be careful. She carried over her arm a black bag, from which she now drew several packets carefully wrapped in paper. Three of these she selected, replacing the others in the bag. Two of the packets she mixed together and then she cautiously opened the third.

"Better stand back, your Majesty," she advised, "for if this powder falls on you you might be transformed yourself."

The King hastily retreated to the end of the room. As Blinkie mixed the third powder with the others she waved her hands over it, mumbled a few words, and then backed away as quickly as she could.

Cap'n Bill was slumbering peacefully, all unconscious of what was going on. Puff! A great cloud of smoke rolled over the bed and completely hid him from view. When the smoke rolled away, both Blinkie and the King saw that the body of the stranger had quite disappeared, while in his place, crouching in the middle of the bed, was a little gray grasshopper.

One curious thing about this grasshopper was that the last joint of its left leg was made of wood. Another curious thing — considering it was a grasshopper — was that it began talking, crying out in a tiny but sharp voice:

"Here — you people! What do you mean by treating me so? Put me back where I belong, at once, or you'll be sorry!"

The cruel King turned pale at hearing the grasshopper's threats, but the Wicked Witch merely

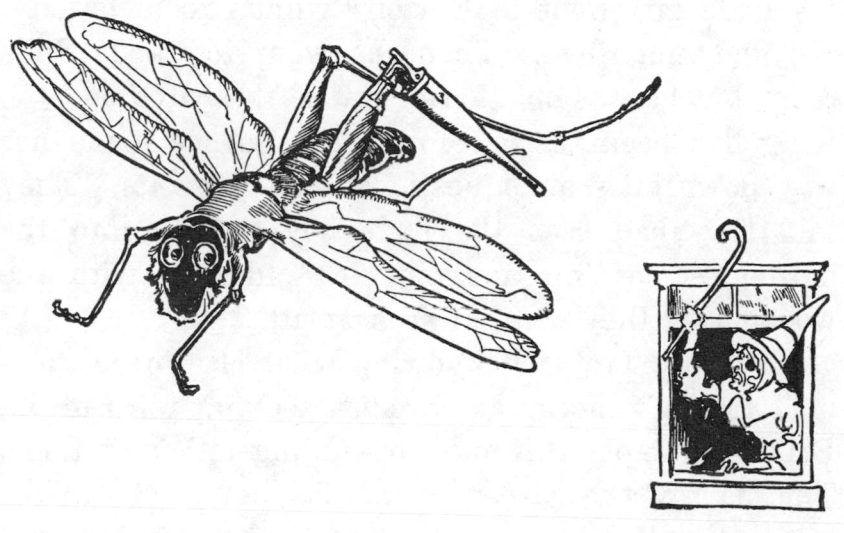

laughed in derision. Then she raised her stick and aimed a vicious blow at the grasshopper, but before the stick struck the bed the tiny hopper made a marvelous jump — marvelous, indeed, when we consider that it had a wooden leg. It rose in the air and sailed across the room and passed right through the open window, where it disappeared from their view.

"Good!" shouted the King. "We are well rid of this desperate wizard." And then they both laughed heartily at the success of the incantation, and went away to complete their horrid plans.

After Trot had visited a time with Princess Gloria, the little girl went to Button-Bright's room but did not find him there. Then she went to Cap'n Bill's room, but he was not there because the witch and the King had been there before her. So she made her way downstairs and questioned the servants. They said they had seen the little boy go out into the garden, some time ago, but the old man with the wooden leg they had not seen at all.

Therefore Trot, not knowing what else to do, rambled through the great gardens, seeking for Button-Bright or Cap'n Bill and not finding either of them. This part of the garden, which lay before the castle, was not walled in, but extended to the roadway, and the paths were open to the edge of the forest; so, after two hours of vain search for her friends, the little girl returned to the castle.

But at the doorway a soldier stopped her.

"I live here," said Trot, "so it's all right to let me in. The King has given me a room."

"Well, he has taken it back again," was the soldier's reply. "His Majesty's orders are to turn you away if you attempt to enter. I am also ordered to forbid the boy, your companion, to again enter the King's castle."

"How 'bout Cap'n Bill?" she inquired.

"Why, it seems he has mysteriously disappeared," replied the soldier, shaking his head ominously. "Where he has gone to, I can't make out, but I can assure you he is no longer in this castle. I'm sorry, little girl, to disappoint you. Don't blame me; I must obey my master's orders."

Now, all her life Trot had been accustomed to depend on Cap'n Bill, so when this good friend was suddenly taken from her she felt very miserable and forlorn indeed. She was brave enough not to cry before the soldier, or even to let him see her grief and anxiety, but after she was turned away from the castle she sought a quiet bench in the garden and for a time sobbed as if her heart would break.

It was Button-Bright who found her, at last, just as the sun had set and the shades of evening were falling. He also had been turned away from the King's castle, when he tried to enter it, and in the park he came across Trot.

"Never mind," said the boy. "We can find a place to sleep."

"I want Cap'n Bill," wailed the girl.

"Well, so do I," was the reply. "But we haven't got him. Where do you s'pose he is, Trot?"

"I don't s'pose anything. He's gone, an' that's all I know 'bout it."

Button-Bright sat on the bench beside her and thrust his hands in the pockets of his knickerbockers. Then he reflected somewhat gravely for him.

"Cap'n Bill isn't around here," he said, letting his eyes wander over the dim garden, "so we must go somewhere else if we want to find him. Besides, it's fast getting dark, and if we want to find a place to sleep we must get busy while we can see where to go."

He rose from the bench as he said this and Trot also jumped up, drying her eyes on her apron. Then she walked beside him out of the grounds of the King's castle. They did not go by the main path, but passed through an opening in a hedge and found themselves in a small but well-worn roadway. Following this for some distance, along a winding way, they came upon no house or building that would afford them refuge for the night. It became so dark

that they could scarcely see their way, and finally Trot stopped and suggested that they camp under a tree.

"All right," said Button-Bright, "I've often found that leaves make a good warm blanket. But — look there, Trot! — isn't that a light flashing over yonder?"

"It certainly is, Button-Bright. Let's go over and see if it's a house. Whoever lives there couldn't treat us worse than the King did."

To reach the light they had to leave the road, so they stumbled over hillocks and brushwood, hand in hand, keeping the tiny speck of light always in sight.

They were rather forlorn little waifs, outcasts in a strange country and forsaken by their only friend and guardian, Cap'n Bill. So they were very glad when finally they reached a small cottage and, looking in through its one window, saw Pon, the gardener's boy, sitting by a fire of twigs.

As Trot opened the door and walked boldly in, Pon sprang up to greet them. They told him of Cap'n Bill's disappearance and how they had been turned out of the King's castle. As they finished the story Pon shook his head sadly.

"King Krewl is plotting mischief, I fear," said he, "for to-day he sent for old Blinkie, the Wicked

# Chapter Twelve

Witch, and with my own eyes I saw her come from the castle and hobble away toward her hut. She had been with the King and Googly-Goo, and I was afraid they were going to work some enchantment on Gloria so she would no longer love me. But perhaps the witch was only called to the castle to enchant your friend, Cap'n Bill."

"Could she do that?" asked Trot, horrified by the suggestion.

"I suppose so, for old Blinkie can do a lot of wicked magical things."

"What sort of an enchantment could she put on Cap'n Bill?"

"I don't know. But he has disappeared, so I'm pretty certain she has done something dreadful to him. But don't worry. If it has happened, it can't be helped, and if it hasn't happened we may be able to find him in the morning."

With this Pon went to the cupboard and brought food for them. Trot was far too worried to eat, but Button-Bright made a good supper from the simple food and then lay down before the fire and went to sleep. The little girl and the gardener's boy, however, sat for a long time staring into the fire, busy with their thoughts. But at last Trot, too, became sleepy and Pon gently covered her with the one blanket he possessed. Then he threw more wood on the fire and laid himself down before it, next to Button-Bright. Soon all three were fast asleep. They were in a good deal of trouble; but they were young, and sleep was good to them because for a time it made them forget.

## CHAPTER 13

# Glinda the Good and the Scarecrow of Oz

That country south of the Emerald City, in the Land of Oz, is known as the Quadling Country, and in the very southernmost part of it stands a splendid palace in which lives Glinda the Good.

Glinda is the Royal Sorceress of Oz. She has wonderful magical powers and uses them only to benefit the subjects of Ozma's kingdom. Even the famous Wizard of Oz pays tribute to her, for Glinda taught him all the real magic he knows, and she is his superior in all sorts of sorcery.

Everyone loves Glinda, from the dainty and exquisite Ruler, Ozma, down to the humblest inhabitant of Oz, for she is always kindly and helpful and willing to listen to their troubles, however busy she may be. No one knows her age, but all can see how beautiful and stately she is. Her hair is like red gold and finer than the finest silken strands. Her eyes are blue as the sky and always frank and smiling. Her cheeks are the envy of peach-blows and her mouth is enticing as a rosebud. Glinda is tall and wears splendid gowns that trail behind her as she walks. She wears no jewels, for her beauty would shame them.

For attendants Glinda has half a hundred of the loveliest girls in Oz. They are gathered from all over Oz, from among the Winkies, the Munchkins, the Gillikins and the Quadlings, as well as from Ozma's magnificent Emerald City, and it is considered a great favor to be allowed to serve the Royal Sorceress.

Among the many wonderful things in Glinda's palace is the Great Book of Records. In this book is inscribed everything that takes place in all the world, just the instant it happens; so that by referring to its pages Glinda knows what is taking place far and near, in every country that exists. In this way she learns when and where she can help any in distress or danger, and although her duties are confined

The most popular
man in all the
Land of Oz

to assisting those who inhabit the Land of Oz, she is always interested in what takes place in the unprotected outside world.

So it was that on a certain evening Glinda sat in her library, surrounded by a bevy of her maids, who were engaged in spinning, weaving and embroidery, when an attendant announced the arrival at the palace of the Scarecrow.

This personage was one of the most famous and popular in all the Land of Oz. His body was merely a suit of Munchkin clothes stuffed with straw, but his head was a round sack filled with bran, with which the Wizard of Oz had mixed some magic brains of a very superior sort. The eyes, nose and mouth of the Scarecrow were painted upon the front of the sack, as were his ears, and since this quaint being had been endowed with life, the expression of his face was very interesting, if somewhat comical.

The Scarecrow was good all through, even to his brains, and while he was naturally awkward in his movements and lacked the neat symmetry of other people, his disposition was so kind and considerate and he was so obliging and honest, that all who knew him loved him, and there were few people in Oz who had not met our Scarecrow and made his acquaintance.

He lived part of the time in Ozma's palace at the Emerald City, part of the time in his own corncob castle in the Winkie Country, and part of the time he traveled over all Oz, visiting with the people and playing with the children, whom he dearly loved.

It was on one of his wandering journeys that the Scarecrow had arrived at Glinda's palace, and the Sorceress at once made him welcome. As he sat beside her, talking of his adventures, he asked:

"What's new in the way of news?"

Glinda opened her Great Book of Records and read some of the last pages.

"Here is an item quite curious and interesting," she announced, an accent of surprise in her voice. "Three people from the big Outside World have arrived in Jinxland."

"Where is Jinxland?" inquired the Scarecrow.

"Very near here, a little to the east of us," she said. "In fact, Jinxland is a little slice taken off the Quadling Country, but separated from it by a range of high mountains, at the foot of which lies a wide, deep gulf that is supposed to be impassable."

"Then Jinxland is really a part of the Land of Oz," said he.

"Yes," returned Glinda, "but Oz people know nothing of it, except what is recorded here in my book."

"What does the Book say about it?" asked the Scarecrow.

"It is ruled by a wicked man called King Krewl, although he has no right to the title. Most of the people are good, but they are very timid and live in constant fear of their fierce ruler. There are also several Wicked Witches who keep the inhabitants of Jinxland in a state of terror."

"Do those witches have any magical powers?" inquired the Scarecrow.

"Yes, they seem to understand witchcraft in its most evil form, for one of them has just transformed a respectable and honest old sailor — one of the strangers who arrived there — into a grasshopper. This same witch, Blinkie by name, is also planning to freeze the heart of a beautiful Jinxland girl named Princess Gloria."

"Why, that's a dreadful thing to do!" exclaimed the Scarecrow.

Glinda's face was very grave. She read in her book how Trot and Button-Bright were turned out of the King's castle, and how they found refuge in the hut of Pon, the gardener's boy.

"I'm afraid those helpless earth people will endure

much suffering in Jinxland, even if the wicked King and the witches permit them to live," said the good Sorceress, thoughtfully. "I wish I might help them."

"Can I do anything?" asked the Scarecrow, anxiously. "If so, tell me what to do, and I'll do it."

For a few moments Glinda did not reply, but sat musing over the records. Then she said: "I am going to send you to Jinxland, to protect Trot and Button-Bright and Cap'n Bill."

"All right," answered the Scarecrow in a cheerful voice. "I know Button-Bright already, for he has been in the Land of Oz before. You remember he went away from the Land of Oz in one of our Wizard's big bubbles."

"Yes," said Glinda, "I remember that." Then she carefully instructed the Scarecrow what to do and gave him certain magical things which he placed in the pockets of his ragged Munchkin coat.

"As you have no need to sleep," said she, "you may as well start at once."

"The night is the same as day to me," he replied, "except that I cannot see my way so well in the dark."

"I will furnish a light to guide you," promised the Sorceress.

So the Scarecrow bade her good-bye and at once started on his journey. By morning he had reached the mountains that separated the Quadling Country from Jinxland. The sides of these mountains were too steep to climb, but the Scarecrow took a small rope from his pocket and tossed one end upward, into the air. The rope unwound itself for hundreds of feet, until it caught upon a peak of rock at the very top of a mountain, for it was a magic rope furnished him by Glinda. The Scarecrow climbed the rope and, after pulling it up, let it down on the other side of the mountain range. When he descended the rope on this

side he found himself in Jinxland, but at his feet
yawned the Great Gulf, which must be crossed before
he could proceed any farther.

The Scarecrow knelt down and examined the
ground carefully, and in a moment he discovered a
fuzzy brown spider that had rolled itself into a ball.
So he took two tiny pills from his pocket and laid
them beside the spider, which unrolled itself and
quickly ate up the pills. Then the Scarecrow said in
a voice of command:

"Spin!" and the spider obeyed instantly.

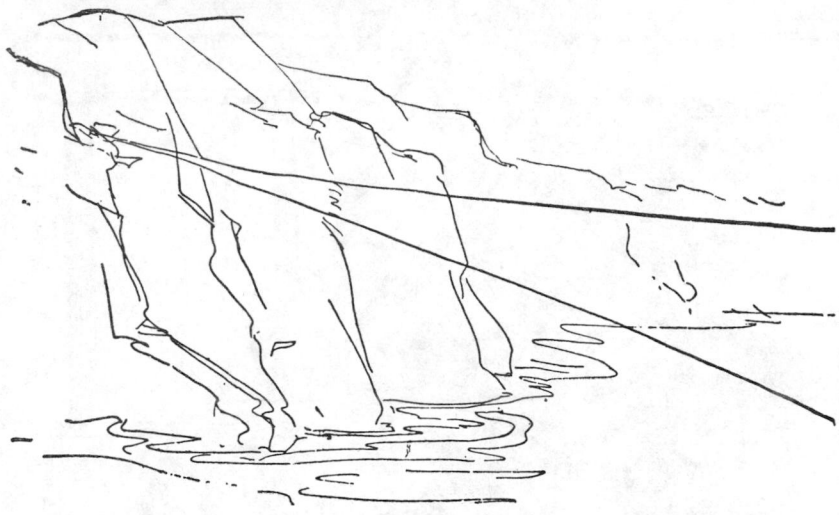

In a few moments the little creature had spun two
slender but strong strands that reached way across the

gulf, one being five or six feet above the other. When these were completed the Scarecrow started across the tiny bridge, walking upon one strand as a person walks upon a rope, and holding to the upper strand with his hands to prevent him from losing his balance and toppling over into the gulf. The tiny threads held him safely, thanks to the strength given them by the magic pills.

Presently he was safe across and standing on the plains of Jinxland. Far away he could see the towers of the King's castle and toward this he at once began to walk.

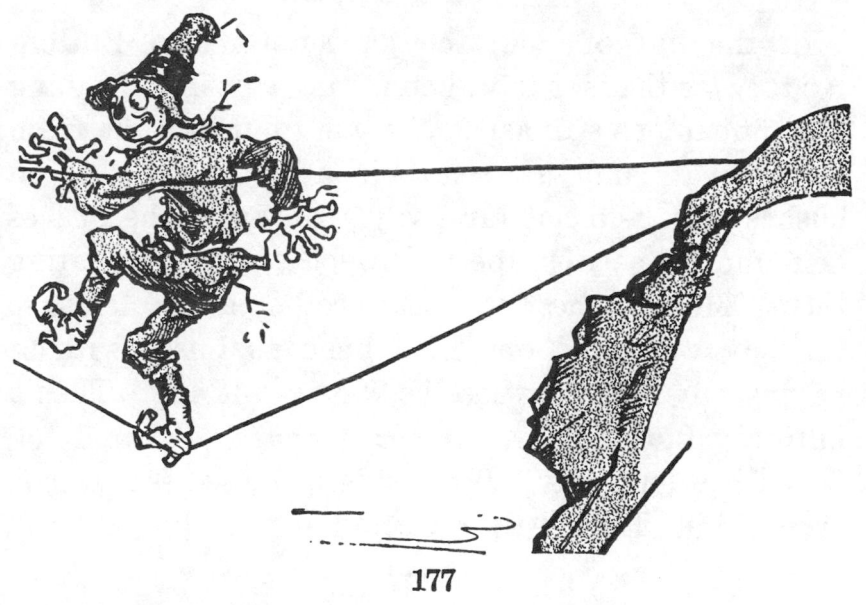

## CHAPTER 14

# The Frozen Heart

In the hut of Pon, the gardener's boy, Button-Bright was the first to waken in the morning. Leaving his companions still asleep, he went out into the fresh morning air and saw some blackberries growing on bushes in a field not far away. Going to the bushes he found the berries ripe and sweet, so he began eating them. More bushes were scattered over the fields, so the boy wandered on, from bush to bush, without paying any heed to where he was wandering. Then a butterfly fluttered by. He gave chase to it and followed it a long way. When finally he paused to look around him, Button-Bright could see no sign of Pon's house, nor had he the slightest idea in which direction it lay.

"Well, I'm lost again," he remarked to himself. "But never mind; I've been lost lots of times. Some-one is sure to find me."

Trot was a little worried about Button-Bright when she awoke and found him gone. Knowing how care-less he was, she believed that he had strayed away, but felt that he would come back in time, because he had a habit of not staying lost. Pon got the little girl some food for her breakfast and then together they went out of the hut and stood in the sunshine.

Pon's house was some distance off the road, but they could see it from where they stood and both gave a start of surprise when they discovered two soldiers walking along the roadway and escorting Princess Gloria between them. The poor girl had her hands bound together, to prevent her from struggling, and the soldiers rudely dragged her forward when her steps seemed to lag.

Behind this group came King Krewl, wearing his jeweled crown and swinging in his hand a slender golden staff with a ball of clustered gems at one end.

"Where are they going?" asked Trot.

"To the house of the Wicked Witch, I fear," Pon

replied. "Come, let us follow them, for I am sure they intend to harm my dear Gloria."

"Won't they see us?" she asked timidly.

"We won't let them. I know a short cut through the trees to Blinkie's house," said he.

So they hurried away through the trees and reached the house of the witch ahead of the King and his soldiers. Hiding themselves in the shrubbery, they watched the approach of poor Gloria and her escort, all of whom passed so near to them that Pon could have put out a hand and touched his sweetheart, had he dared to.

Blinkie's house had eight sides, with a door and a window in each side. Smoke was coming out of the chimney and as the guards brought Gloria to one of the doors it was opened by the old witch in person. She chuckled with evil glee and rubbed her skinny hands together to show the delight with which she greeted her victim, for Blinkie was pleased to be able to perform her wicked rites on one so fair and sweet as the Princess.

Gloria struggled to resist when they bade her enter the house, so the soldiers forced her through the doorway and even the King gave her a shove as he followed close behind. Pon was so incensed at the cruelty shown Gloria that he forgot all caution and rushed forward to enter the house also; but one of the soldiers prevented him, pushing the gardener's boy away with violence and slamming the door in his face.

"Never mind," said Trot soothingly, as Pon rose from where he had fallen. "You couldn't do much to help the poor Princess if you were inside. How unfortunate it is that you are in love with her!"

"True," he answered sadly, "it is indeed my misfortune. If I did not love her, it would be none of my business what the King did to his niece Gloria; but the unlucky circumstance of my loving her makes it my duty to defend her."

"I don't see how you can, duty or no duty," observed Trot.

"No; I am powerless, for they are stronger than I. But we might peek in through the window and see what they are doing."

Trot was somewhat curious, too, so they crept up to one of the windows and looked in, and it so happened that those inside the witch's house were so busy they did not notice that Pon and Trot were watching them.

Gloria had been tied to a stout post in the center of

the room and the King was giving the Wicked Witch a quantity of money and jewels, which Googly-Goo had provided in payment. When this had been done the King said to her:

"Are you perfectly sure you can freeze this maiden's heart, so that she will no longer love that low gardener's boy?"

"Sure as witchcraft, your Majesty," the creature replied.

"Then get to work," said the King. "There may be some unpleasant features about the ceremony that would annoy me, so I'll bid you good day and leave you to carry out your contract. One word, however: If you fail, I shall burn you at the stake!" Then he beckoned to his soldiers to follow him, and throwing wide the door of the house walked out.

This action was so sudden that King Krewl almost caught Trot and Pon eavesdropping, but they managed to run around the house before he saw them. Away he marched, up the road, followed by his men, heartlessly leaving Gloria to the mercies of old Blinkie.

When they again crept up to the window, Trot and Pon saw Blinkie gloating over her victim. Although nearly fainting from fear, the proud Princess gazed

with haughty defiance into the face of the wicked creature; but she was bound so tightly to the post that she could do no more to express her loathing.

Pretty soon Blinkie went to a kettle that was swinging by a chain over the fire and tossed into it several magical compounds. The kettle gave three flashes, and at every flash another witch appeared in the room.

These hags were very ugly but when one-eyed Blinkie whispered her orders to them they grinned with joy as they began dancing around Gloria. First one and then another cast something into the kettle, when to the astonishment of the watchers at the window all three of the old women were instantly transformed into maidens of exquisite beauty, dressed in the daintiest costumes imaginable. Only their eyes could not be disguised, and an evil glare still shone in their depths. But if the eyes were cast down or hidden, one could not help but admire these beautiful creatures, even with the knowledge that they were mere illusions of witchcraft.

Trot certainly admired them, for she had never seen anything so dainty and bewitching, but her attention was quickly drawn to their deeds instead of their persons, and then horror replaced admiration.

Into the kettle old Blinkie poured another mess

from a big brass bottle she took from a chest, and this made the kettle begin to bubble and smoke violently. One by one the beautiful witches approached to stir the contents of the kettle and to mutter a magic charm. Their movements were graceful and rhythmic and the Wicked Witch who had called them to her aid watched them with an evil grin upon her wrinkled face.

Finally the incantation was complete. The kettle ceased bubbling and together the witches lifted it from the fire. Then Blinkie brought a wooden ladle and filled it from the contents of the kettle. Going with the spoon to Princess Gloria she cried:

"Love no more! Magic art
Now will freeze your mortal heart!"

With this she dashed the contents of the ladle full upon Gloria's breast.

Trot saw the body of the Princess become transparent, so that her beating heart showed plainly. But now the heart turned from a vivid red to gray, and then to white. A layer of frost formed about it and tiny icicles clung to its surface. Then slowly the body of the girl became visible again and the heart was hidden from view. Gloria seemed to have fainted, but now she recovered and, opening her beautiful eyes, stared coldly and without emotion at the group of witches confronting her.

Blinkie and the others knew by that one cold look that their charm had been successful. They burst into a chorus of wild laughter and the three beautiful ones began dancing again, while Blinkie unbound the Princess and set her free.

Trot rubbed her eyes to prove that she was wide awake and seeing clearly, for her astonishment was great when the three lovely maidens turned into ugly, crooked hags again, leaning on broomsticks and canes. They jeered at Gloria, but the Princess regarded them with cold disdain. Being now free, she walked to a door, opened it and passed out. And the witches let her go.

Trot and Pon had been so intent upon this scene that in their eagerness they had pressed quite hard against the window. Just as Gloria went out of the house the window-sash broke loose from its fastenings and fell with a crash into the room. The witches uttered a chorus of screams and then, seeing that their magical incantation had been observed, they rushed for the open window with uplifted broomsticks and canes. But Pon was off like the wind, and Trot

followed at his heels. Fear lent them strength to run, to leap across ditches, to speed up the hills and to vault the low fences as a deer would.

The band of witches had dashed through the window in pursuit; but Blinkie was so old, and the others so crooked and awkward, that they soon realized they would be unable to overtake the fugitives. So the three who had been summoned by the Wicked Witch put their canes or broomsticks between their legs and flew away through the air, quickly disappearing against the blue sky. Blinkie, however, was so enraged at Pon and Trot that she hobbled on in the direction they had taken, fully determined to catch them, in time, and to punish them terribly for spying upon her witchcraft.

When Pon and Trot had run so far that they were confident they had made good their escape, they sat down near the edge of a forest to get their breath again, for both were panting hard from their exertions. Trot was the first to recover speech, and she said to her companion:

" My! wasn't it terr'ble? "

" The most terrible thing I ever saw," Pon agreed.

" And they froze Gloria's heart; so now she can't love you any more."

"Well, they froze her heart, to be sure," admitted Pon, "but I'm in hopes I can melt it with my love."

"Where do you s'pose Gloria is?" asked the girl, after a pause.

"She left the witch's house just before we did. Perhaps she has gone back to the King's castle," he said.

"I'm pretty sure she started off in a diff'rent direction," declared Trot. "I looked over my shoulder, as I ran, to see how close the witches were, and I'm sure I saw Gloria walking slowly away toward the north."

"Then let us circle around that way," proposed Pon, "and perhaps we shall meet her."

Trot agreed to this and they left the grove and began to circle around toward the north, thus drawing nearer and nearer to old Blinkie's house again. The Wicked Witch did not suspect this change of direction, so when she came to the grove she passed through it and continued on.

Pon and Trot had reached a place less than half a mile from the witch's house when they saw Gloria walking toward them. The Princess moved with great dignity and with no show of haste whatever, holding her head high and looking neither to right nor left.

Pon rushed forward, holding out his arms as if to embrace her and calling her sweet names. But Gloria gazed upon him coldly and repelled him with a haughty gesture. At this the poor gardener's boy sank upon his knees and hid his face in his arms, weeping bitter tears; but the Princess was not at all moved by his distress. Passing him by, she drew her skirts aside, as if unwilling they should touch him, and then she walked up the path a way and hesitated, as if uncertain where to go next.

Trot was grieved by Pon's sobs and indignant because Gloria treated him so badly. But she remembered why.

"I guess your heart is frozen, all right," she said to the Princess. Gloria nodded gravely, in reply, and then turned her back upon the little girl. "Can't you like even me?" asked Trot, half pleadingly.

"No," said Gloria.

"Your voice sounds like a refrig'rator," sighed the little girl. "I'm awful sorry for you, 'cause you were sweet an' nice to me before this happened. You can't help it, of course; but it's a dreadful thing, jus' the same."

"My heart is frozen to all mortal loves," announced Gloria, calmly. "I do not love even myself."

"That's too bad," said Trot, "for, if you can't love anybody, you can't expect anybody to love you."

"I do!" cried Pon. "I shall always love her."

"Well, you're just a gardener's boy," replied Trot, "and I didn't think you 'mounted to much, from the first. I can love the old Princess Gloria, with a warm heart an' nice manners, but this one gives me the shivers."

"It's her icy heart, that's all," said Pon.

"That's enough," insisted Trot. "Seeing her heart isn't big enough to skate on, I can't see that she's of any use to anyone. For my part, I'm goin' to try to find Button-Bright an' Cap'n Bill."

"I will go with you," decided Pon. "It is evident that Gloria no longer loves me and that her heart is frozen too stiff for me to melt it with my own love; therefore I may as well help you to find your friends."

As Trot started off, Pon cast one more imploring look at the Princess, who returned it with a chilly stare. So he followed after the little girl.

As for the Princess, she hesitated a moment and then turned in the same direction the others had taken, but going far more slowly. Soon she heard footsteps pattering behind her, and up came Googly-Goo. a little out of breath with running.

# Chapter Fourteen

"Stop, Gloria!" he cried. "I have come to take you back to my mansion, where we are to be married."

She looked at him wonderingly a moment, then tossed her head disdainfully and walked on. But Googly-Goo kept beside her.

"What does this mean?" he demanded. "Haven't you discovered that you no longer love that gardener's boy, who stood in my way?"

"Yes; I have discovered it," she replied. "My heart is frozen to all mortal loves. I cannot love you, or Pon, or the cruel King my uncle, or even myself. Go your way, Googly-Goo, for I will wed no one at all."

He stopped in dismay when he heard this, but in another minute he exclaimed angrily:

"You *must* wed me, Princess Gloria, whether you want to or not! I paid to have your heart frozen; I also paid the King to permit our marriage. If you now refuse me it will mean that I have been robbed — robbed — robbed of my precious money and jewels!"

He almost wept with despair, but she laughed a cold, bitter laugh and passed on. Googly-Goo caught at her arm, as if to restrain her, but she whirled and dealt him a blow that sent him reeling into a ditch beside the path. Here he lay for a long time, half covered by muddy water, dazed with surprise.

Finally the old courtier arose, dripping, and climbed from the ditch. The Princess had gone; so, muttering threats of vengeance upon her, upon the King and upon Blinkie, old Googly-Goo hobbled back to his mansion to have the mud removed from his costly velvet clothes.

# Trot Meets the Scarecrow

Trot and Pon covered many leagues of ground, searching through forests, in fields and in many of the little villages of Jinxland, but could find no trace of either Cap'n Bill or Button-Bright. Finally they paused beside a cornfield and sat upon a stile to rest. Pon took some apples from his pocket and gave one to Trot. Then he began eating another himself, for this was their time for luncheon. When his apple was finished Pon tossed the core into the field.

"Tchuk-tchuk!" said a strange voice. "What do you mean by hitting me in the eye with an apple-core?"

# The Scarecrow of Oz

Then rose up the form of the Scarecrow, who had hidden himself in the cornfield while he examined Pon and Trot and decided whether they were worthy to be helped.

"Excuse me," said Pon. "I didn't know you were there."

"How did you happen to be there, anyhow?" asked Trot.

The Scarecrow came forward with awkward steps and stood beside them.

"Ah, you are the gardener's boy," he said to Pon. Then he turned to Trot. "And you are the little girl who came to Jinxland riding on a big bird, and who has had the misfortune to lose her friend, Cap'n Bill, and her chum, Button-Bright."

"Why, how did you know all that?" she inquired.

"I know a lot of things," replied the Scarecrow, winking at her comically. "My brains are the Carefully-Assorted, Double-Distilled, High-Efficiency sort that the Wizard of Oz makes. He admits, himself, that my brains are the best he ever manufactured."

"I think I've heard of you," said Trot slowly, as she looked the Scarecrow over with much interest; "but you used to live in the Land of Oz."

"Oh, I do now," he replied cheerfully. "I've just

come over the mountains from the Quadling Country to see if I can be of any help to you."

"Who, me?" asked Pon.

"No, the strangers from the big world. It seems they need looking after."

"I'm doing that myself," said Pon, a little ungraciously. "If you will pardon me for saying so, I don't see how a Scarecrow with painted eyes can look after anyone."

"If you don't see that, you are more blind than the Scarecrow," asserted Trot. "He's a fairy man, Pon, and comes from the fairyland of Oz, so he can do 'most anything. I hope," she added, turning to the Scarecrow, "you can find Cap'n Bill for me."

"I will try, anyhow," he promised. "But who is that old woman who is running toward us and shaking her stick at us?"

Trot and Pon turned around and both uttered an exclamation of fear. The next instant they took to their heels and ran fast up the path. For it was old Blinkie, the Wicked Witch, who had at last traced them to this place. Her anger was so great that she was determined not to abandon the chase of Pon and Trot until she had caught and punished them.

The Scarecrow understood at once that the old

woman meant harm to his new friends, so as she drew
near he stepped before her. His appearance was so
sudden and unexpected that Blinkie ran into him
and toppled him over, but she tripped on his straw
body and went rolling in the path beside him.

The Scarecrow sat up and said: "I beg your pardon!" but she whacked him with her stick and
knocked him flat again. Then, furious with rage, the
old witch sprang upon her victim and began pulling
the straw out of his body. The poor Scarecrow was
helpless to resist and in a few moments all that was

left of him was an empty suit of clothes and a heap of straw beside it. Fortunately, Blinkie did not harm his head, for it rolled into a little hollow and escaped her notice. Fearing that Pon and Trot would escape her, she quickly resumed the chase and disappeared over the brow of a hill, following the direction in which she had seen them go.

Only a short time elapsed before a gray grasshopper with a wooden leg came hopping along and lit directly on the upturned face of the Scarecrow's head.

"Pardon me, but you are resting yourself upon my nose," remarked the Scarecrow.

"Oh! are you alive?" asked the grasshopper.

"That is a question I have never been able to decide," said the Scarecrow's head. "When my body is properly stuffed I have animation and can move around as well as any live person. The brains in the head you are now occupying as a throne, are of very superior quality and do a lot of very clever thinking. But whether that is being alive, or not, I cannot prove to you; for one who lives is liable to death, while I am only liable to destruction."

"Seems to me," said the grasshopper, rubbing his nose with his front legs, "that in your case it doesn't matter — unless you're destroyed already."

"I am not; all I need is re-stuffing," declared the Scarecrow; "and if Pon and Trot escape the witch, and come back here, I am sure they will do me that favor."

"Tell me! Are Trot and Pon around here?" inquired the grasshopper, its small voice trembling with excitement.

The Scarecrow did not answer at once, for both his eyes were staring straight upward at a beautiful face that was slightly bent over his head. It was, indeed, Princess Gloria, who had wandered to this spot, very much surprised when she heard the Scarecrow's head talk and the tiny gray grasshopper answer it.

"This," said the Scarecrow, still staring at her, "must be the Princess who loves Pon, the gardener's boy."

"Oh, indeed!" exclaimed the grasshopper — who of course was Cap'n Bill — as he examined the young lady curiously.

"No," said Gloria frigidly, "I do not love Pon, or anyone else, for the Wicked Witch has frozen my heart.'

"What a shame!" cried the Scarecrow. "One so lovely should be able to love. But would you mind, my dear, stuffing that straw into my body again?"

The dainty Princess glanced at the straw and at the well-worn blue Munchkin clothes and shrank back in disdain. But she was spared from refusing the Scarecrow's request by the appearance of Trot and Pon, who had hidden in some bushes just over the brow of the hill and waited until old Blinkie had

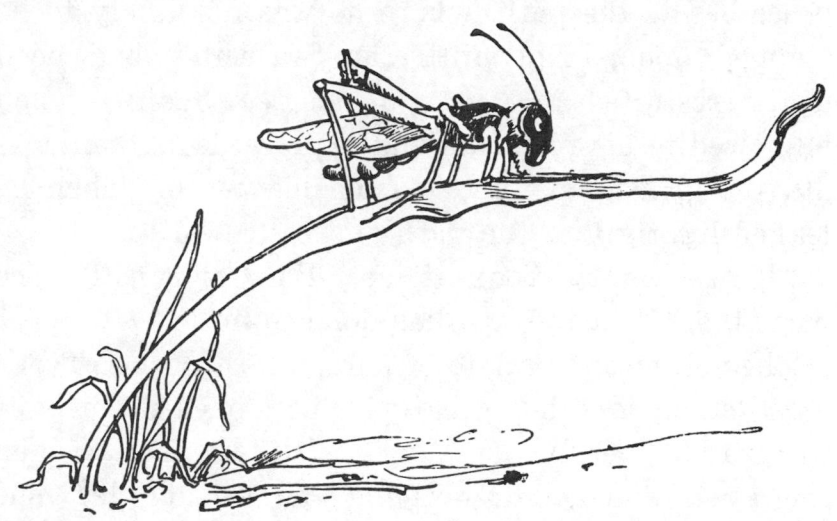

passed them by. Their hiding place was on the same side as the witch's blind eye, and she rushed on in the chase of the girl and the youth without being aware that they had tricked her.

Trot was shocked at the Scarecrow's sad condition and at once began putting the straw back into his body. Pon, at sight of Gloria, again appealed to her to take pity on him, but the frozen-hearted Princess turned coldly away and with a sigh the gardener's boy began to assist Trot.

Neither of them at first noticed the small grasshopper, which at their appearance had skipped off the Scarecrow's nose and was now clinging to a wisp of grass beside the path, where he was not likely to be stepped upon. Not until the Scarecrow had been neatly restuffed and set upon his feet again — when he bowed to his restorers and expressed his thanks — did the grasshopper move from his perch. Then he leaped lightly into the path and called out:

"Trot — Trot! Look at me. I'm Cap'n Bill! See what the Wicked Witch has done to me."

The voice was small, to be sure, but it reached Trot's ears and startled her greatly. She looked intently at the grasshopper, her eyes wide with fear at first; then she knelt down and, noticing the wooden leg, she began to weep sorrowfully.

"Oh, Cap'n Bill — dear Cap'n Bill! What a cruel thing to do!" she sobbed.

"Don't cry, Trot," begged the grasshopper. "It didn't hurt any, and it doesn't hurt now. But it's mighty inconvenient an' humiliatin', to say the least."

"I wish," said the girl indignantly, while trying

hard to restrain her tears, " that I was big 'nough an' strong 'nough to give that horrid witch a good beating. She ought to be turned into a toad for doing this to you, Cap'n Bill! "

" Never mind," urged the Scarecrow, in a comforting voice, " such a transformation doesn't last always, and as a general thing there's some way to break the enchantment. I'm sure Glinda could do it, in a jiffy."

" Who is Glinda?" inquired Cap'n Bill.

Then the Scarecrow told them all about Glinda, not forgetting to mention her beauty and goodness and her wonderful powers of magic. He also explained how the Royal Sorceress had sent him to Jinxland especially to help the strangers, whom she knew to be in danger because of the wiles of the cruel King and the Wicked Witch.

## CHAPTER 16

# Pon Summons the King to Surrender

Gloria had drawn near to the group to listen to their talk, and it seemed to interest her in spite of her frigid manner. They knew, of course, that the poor Princess could not help being cold and reserved, so they tried not to blame her.

"I ought to have come here a little sooner," said the Scarecrow, regretfully; "but Glinda sent me as soon as she discovered you were here and were likely to get into trouble. And now that we are all together — except Button-Bright, over whom it is useless to worry — I propose we hold a council of war, to decide what is best to be done."

# Chapter Sixteen

That seemed a wise thing to do, so they all sat down upon the grass, including Gloria, and the grasshopper perched upon Trot's shoulder and allowed her to stroke him gently with her hand.

"In the first place," began the Scarecrow, "this King Krewl is a usurper and has no right to rule this Kingdom of Jinxland."

"That is true," said Pon, eagerly. "My father was King before him, and I —"

"You are a gardener's boy," interrupted the Scarecrow. "Your father had no right to rule, either, for the rightful King of this land was the father of Princess Gloria, and only she is entitled to sit upon the throne of Jinxland."

"Good!" exclaimed Trot. "But what'll we do with King Krewl? I s'pose he won't give up the throne unless he has to."

"No, of course not," said the Scarecrow. "Therefore it will be our duty to *make* him give up the throne."

"How?" asked Trot.

"Give me time to think," was the reply. "That's what my brains are for. I don't know whether you people ever think, or not, but my brains are the best that the Wizard of Oz ever turned out, and if I give them plenty of time to work, the result usually surprises me."

"Take your time, then," suggested Trot. "There's no hurry."

"Thank you," said the straw man, and sat perfectly still for half an hour. During this interval the grasshopper whispered in Trot's ear, to which he was very close, and Trot whispered back to the grasshopper sitting upon her shoulder. Pon cast loving glances at Gloria, who paid not the slightest heed to them.

Finally the Scarecrow laughed aloud.

"Brains working?" inquired Trot.

"Yes. They seem in fine order to-day. We will conquer King Krewl and put Gloria upon his throne as Queen of Jinxland."

"Fine!" cried the little girl, clapping her hands together gleefully. "But how?"

"Leave the *how* to me," said the Scarecrow proudly. "As a conqueror I'm a wonder. We will, first of all, write a message to send to King Krewl, asking him to surrender. If he refuses, then we will make him surrender."

"Why ask him. when we *know* he'll refuse?" inquired Pon.

"Why, we must be polite, whatever we do,"

explained the Scarecrow. "It would be very rude to conquer a King without proper notice."

They found it difficult to write a message without paper, pen and ink, none of which was at hand; so i was decided to send Pon as a messenger, with instructions to ask the King, politely but firmly, to surrender.

Pon was not anxious to be the messenger. Indeed, he hinted that it might prove a dangerous mission.

# The Scarecrow of Oz

But the Scarecrow was now the acknowledged head of the Army of Conquest, and he would listen to no refusal. So off Pon started for the King's castle, and the others accompanied him as far as his hut, where they had decided to await the gardener's boy's return.

I think it was because Pon had known the Scarecrow such a short time that he lacked confidence in the straw man's wisdom. It was easy to say: "We will conquer King Krewl," but when Pon drew near to the great castle he began to doubt the ability of a straw-stuffed man, a girl, a grasshopper and a frozen-hearted Princess to do it. As for himself, he had never thought of defying the King before.

That was why the gardener's boy was not very bold when he entered the castle and passed through to the enclosed court where the King was just then seated, with his favorite courtiers around him. None prevented Pon's entrance, because he was known to be the gardener's boy, but when the King saw him he began to frown fiercely. He considered Pon to be to blame for all his trouble with Princess Gloria, who since her heart had been frozen had escaped to some unknown place, instead of returning to the castle to wed Googly-Goo, as she had been expected to do. So the King bared his teeth angrily as he demanded:

"What have you done with Princess Gloria?"

"Nothing, your Majesty! I have done nothing at all," answered Pon in a faltering voice. "She does not love me any more and even refuses to speak to me."

"Then why are you here, you rascal?" roared the King.

Pon looked first one way and then another, but saw no means of escape; so he plucked up courage.

"I am here to summon your Majesty to surrender."

"What!" shouted the King. "Surrender? Surrender to whom?"

Pon's heart sank to his boots.

"To the Scarecrow," he replied.

Some of the courtiers began to titter, but King Krewl was greatly annoyed. He sprang up and began to beat poor Pon with the golden staff he carried. Pon howled lustily and would have run away had not two of the soldiers held him until his Majesty was exhausted with punishing the boy. Then they let him go and he left the castle and returned along the road, sobbing at every step because his body was so sore and aching.

"Well," said the Scarecrow, "did the King surrender?"

"No; but he gave me a good drubbing!" sobbed poor Pon.

Trot was very sorry for Pon, but Gloria did not seem affected in any way by her lover's anguish. The grasshopper leaped to the Scarecrow's shoulder and asked him what he was going to do next.

"Conquer," was the reply. "But I will go alone, this time, for beatings cannot hurt me at all; nor can lance thrusts — or sword cuts — or arrow pricks."

"Why is that?" inquired Trot.

"Because I have no nerves, such as you meat people possess. Even grasshoppers have nerves, but straw doesn't; so whatever they do — except just one thing — they cannot injure me. Therefore I expect to conquer King Krewl with ease."

"What is that one thing you excepted?" asked Trot.

"They will never think of it, so never mind. And now, if you will kindly excuse me for a time, I'll go over to the castle and do my conquering."

"You have no weapons," Pon reminded him.

"True," said the Scarecrow. "But if I carried weapons I might injure someone — perhaps seriously — and that would make me unhappy. I will just borrow that riding-whip, which I see in the corner of your hut, if you don't mind. It isn't exactly proper to walk with a riding-whip, but I trust you will excuse the inconsistency."

Pon handed him the whip and the Scarecrow bowed to all the party and left the hut, proceeding leisurely along the way to the King's castle.

## CHAPTER 17

# The Ork Rescues Button-Bright

I must now tell you what had become of Button-Bright since he wandered away in the morning and got lost. This small boy, as perhaps you have discovered, was almost as destitute of nerves as the Scarecrow. Nothing ever astonished him much; nothing ever worried him or made him unhappy. Good fortune or bad fortune he accepted with a quiet smile, never complaining, whatever happened. This was one reason why Button-Bright was a favorite with all who knew him — and perhaps it was the reason why he so often got into difficulties, or found himself lost.

To-day, as he wandered here and there, over hill and down dale, he missed Trot and Cap'n Bill, of whom he was fond, but nevertheless he was not unhappy. The birds sang merrily and the wildflowers were beautiful and the breeze had a fragrance of new-mown hay.

"The only bad thing about this country is its King," he reflected; "but the country isn't to blame for that."

A prairie-dog stuck its round head out of a mound of earth and looked at the boy with bright eyes.

"Walk around my house, please," it said, "and then you won't harm it or disturb the babies."

"All right," answered Button-Bright, and took care not to step on the mound. He went on, whistling merrily, until a petulant voice cried:

"Oh, stop it! Please stop that noise. It gets on my nerves."

Button-Bright saw an old gray owl sitting in the crotch of a tree, and he replied with a laugh: "All right, old Fussy," and stopped whistling until he had passed out of the owl's hearing. At noon he came to a farmhouse where an aged couple lived. They gave him a good dinner and treated him kindly, but the man was deaf and the woman was dumb, so they could answer no questions to guide him on the way to Pon's house. When he left them he was just as much lost as he had been before.

Every grove of trees he saw from a distance he visited, for he remembered that the King's castle was near a grove of trees and Pon's hut was near the King's castle; but always he met with disappointment. Finally, passing through one of these groves, he came out into the open and found himself face to face with the Ork.

"Hello!" said Button-Bright. "Where did *you* come from?"

"From Orkland," was the reply. "I've found my own country, at last, and it is not far from here, either. I would have come back to you sooner, to see how you are getting along, had not my family and friends welcomed my return so royally that a great celebration was held in my honor. So I couldn't very well leave Orkland again until the excitement was over."

"Can you find your way back home again?" asked the boy.

"Yes, easily; for now I know exactly where it is. But where are Trot and Cap'n Bill?"

Button-Bright related to the Ork their adventures since it had left them in Jinxland, telling of Trot's fear that the King had done something wicked to Cap'n Bill, and of Pon's love for Gloria, and how Trot and Button-Bright had been turned out of the King's castle. That was all the news that the boy had, but it made the Ork anxious for the safety of his friends.

"We must go to them at once, for they may need us," he said.

"I don't know where to go," confessed Button-Bright. "I'm lost."

"Well, I can take you back to the hut of the gardener's boy," promised the Ork, "for when I fly high in the air I can look down and easily spy the King's castle. That was how I happened to spy you, just entering the grove; so I flew down and waited until you came out."

"How can you carry me?" asked the boy.

"You'll have to sit straddle my shoulders and put your arms around my neck. Do you think you can keep from falling off?"

"I'll try," said Button-Bright. So the Ork squatted down and the boy took his seat and held on tight. Then the skinny creature's tail began whirling and up they went, far above all the tree-tops.

After the Ork had circled around once or twice, its sharp eyes located the towers of the castle and away it flew, straight toward the place. As it hovered in the air, near by the castle, Button-Bright pointed out Pon's hut, so they landed just before it and Trot came running out to greet them.

Gloria was introduced to the Ork, who was surprised to find Cap'n Bill transformed into a grasshopper.

"How do you like it?" asked the creature.

"Why, it worries me a good deal," answered Cap'n Bill, perched upon Trot's shoulder. "I'm always afraid o' bein' stepped on, and I don't like the flavor of grass an' can't seem to get used to it. It's my nature to eat grass, you know, but I begin to suspect it's an acquired taste."

" Can you give molasses?" asked the Ork.

"I guess I'm not that kind of a grasshopper," replied Cap'n Bill. " But I can't say what I might do if I was squeezed — which I hope I won't be."

" Well," said the Ork, " it's a great pity, and I'd like to meet that cruel King and his Wicked Witch and punish them both severely. You're awfully small, Cap'n Bill, but I think I would recognize you anywhere by your wooden leg."

Then the Ork and Button-Bright were told all about Gloria's frozen heart and how the Scarecrow had come from the Land of Oz to help them. The Ork seemed rather disturbed when it learned that the Scarecrow had gone alone to conquer King Krewl.

" I'm afraid he'll make a fizzle of it," said the skinny creature, " and there's no telling what that terrible King might do to the poor Scarecrow, who seems like a very interesting person. So I believe I'll take a hand in this conquest myself."

" How?" asked Trot.

" Wait and see," was the reply. " But, first of all, I must fly home again — back to my own country — so if you'll forgive my leaving you so soon, I'll be off at once. Stand away from my tail, please, so that the wind from it, when it revolves, won't knock you over."

They gave the creature plenty of room and away it went like a flash and soon disappeared in the sky.

"I wonder," said Button-Bright, looking solemnly after the Ork, "whether he'll ever come back again."

"Of course he will!" returned Trot. "The Ork's a pretty good fellow, and we can depend on him. An' mark my words, Button-Bright, whenever our Ork does come back, there's one cruel King in Jinxland that'll wish he hadn't."

## CHAPTER 18

# The Scarecrow Meets an Enemy

The Scarecrow was not a bit afraid of King Krewl. Indeed, he rather enjoyed the prospect of conquering the evil King and putting Gloria on the throne of Jinxland in his place. So he advanced boldly to the royal castle and demanded admittance.

Seeing that he was a stranger, the soldiers allowed him to enter. He made his way straight to the throne room, where at that time his Majesty was settling the disputes among his subjects.

"Who are you?" demanded the King.

"I'm the Scarecrow of Oz, and I command you to surrender yourself my prisoner."

"Why should I do that?" inquired the King, much astonished at the straw man's audacity.

"Because I've decided you are too cruel a King to rule so beautiful a country. You must remember that Jinxland is a part of Oz, and therefore you owe allegiance to Ozma of Oz, whose friend and servant I am."

Now, when he heard this, King Krewl was much disturbed in mind, for he knew the Scarecrow spoke the truth. But no one had ever before come to Jinxland from the Land of Oz and the King did not intend to be put out of his throne if he could help it. Therefore he gave a harsh, wicked laugh of derision and said:

"I'm busy, now. Stand out of my way, Scarecrow, and I'll talk with you by and by."

But the Scarecrow turned to the assembled courtiers and people and called in a loud voice:

"I hereby declare, in the name of Ozma of Oz, that this man is no longer ruler of Jinxland. From this moment Princess Gloria is your rightful Queen, and I ask all of you to be loyal to her and to obey her commands."

The people looked fearfully at the King, whom they all hated in their hearts, but likewise feared. Krewl was now in a terrible rage and he raised his golden sceptre and struck the Scarecrow so heavy a blow that he fell to the floor.

But he was up again, in an instant, and with Pon's riding-whip he switched the King so hard that the wicked monarch roared with pain as much as with rage, calling on his soldiers to capture the Scarecrow.

They tried to do that, and thrust their lances and swords into the straw body, but without doing any damage except to make holes in the Scarecrow's clothes. However, they were many against one and finally old Googly-Goo brought a rope which he wound around the Scarecrow, binding his legs together and his arms to his sides, and after that the fight was over.

The King stormed and danced around in a dreadful fury, for he had never been so switched since he was a boy — and perhaps not then. He ordered the Scarecrow thrust into the castle prison, which was no task at all because one man could carry him easily, bound as he was.

Even after the prisoner was removed the King could not control his anger. He tried to figure out some way to be revenged upon the straw man, but could think of nothing that could hurt him.

At last, when the terrified people and the frightened

courtiers had all slunk away, old Googly-Goo approached the king with a malicious grin upon his face.

"I'll tell you what to do," said he. "Build a big bonfire and burn the Scarecrow up, and that will be the end of him."

The King was so delighted with this suggestion that he hugged old Googly-Goo in his joy.

"Of course!" he cried. "The very thing. Why did I not think of it myself?"

So he summoned his soldiers and retainers and bade them prepare a great bonfire in an open space in the castle park. Also he sent word to all his people to assemble and witness the destruction of the Scarecrow who had dared to defy his power. Before long a vast throng gathered in the park and the servants had heaped up enough fuel to make a fire that might be seen for miles away — even in the daytime.

When all was prepared, the King had his throne brought out for him to sit upon and enjoy the spectacle, and then he sent his soldiers to fetch the Scarecrow.

Now the one thing in all the world that the straw man really feared was fire. He knew he would burn very easily and that his ashes wouldn't amount to

much afterward. It wouldn't hurt him to be destroyed in such a manner, but he realized that many people in the Land of Oz, and especially Dorothy and the Royal Ozma, would feel sad if they learned that their old friend the Scarecrow was no longer in existence.

In spite of this, the straw man was brave and faced his fiery fate like a hero. When they marched him out before the concourse of people he turned to the King with great calmness and said:

"This wicked deed will cost you your throne, as well as much suffering, for my friends will avenge my destruction."

"Your friends are not here, nor will they know what I have done to you, when you are gone and cannot tell them," answered the King in a scornful voice.

Then he ordered the Scarecrow bound to a stout stake that he had had driven into the ground, and the materials for the fire were heaped all around him. When this had been done, the King's brass band struck up a lively tune and old Googly-Goo came forward with a lighted match and set fire to the pile.

At once the flames shot up and crept closer and closer toward the Scarecrow. The King and all his people were so intent upon this terrible spectacle

# Chapter Eighteen

that none of them noticed how the sky grew suddenly dark. Perhaps they thought that the loud buzzing sound — like the noise of a dozen moving railway trains — came from the blazing fagots; that the rush of wind was merely a breeze. But suddenly down swept a flock of Orks, half a hundred of them at the least, and the powerful currents of air caused by their revolving tails sent the bonfire scattering in every direction, so that not one burning brand ever touched the Scarecrow.

But that was not the only effect of this sudden tornado. King Krewl was blown out of his throne and went tumbling heels over head until he landed with a bump against the stone wall of his own castle, and before he could rise a big Ork sat upon him and held him pressed flat to the ground. Old Googly-Goo shot up into the air like a rocket and landed on a tree, where he hung by the middle on a high limb, kicking the air with his feet and clawing the air with his hands, and howling for mercy like the coward he was.

The people pressed back until they were jammed close together, while all the soldiers were knocked over and sent sprawling to the earth. The excitement was great for a few minutes, and every frightened inhabitant of Jinxland looked with awe and amazement at the great Orks whose descent had served to rescue the Scarecrow and conquer King Krewl at one and the same time.

The Ork, who was the leader of the band, soon had the Scarecrow free of his bonds. Then he said: " Well, we were just in time to save you, which is better than being a minute too late. You are now the master here, and we are determined to see your orders obeyed."

With this the Ork picked up Krewl's golden crown, which had fallen off his head, and placed it upon the head of the Scarecrow, who in his awkward way then shuffled over to the throne and sat down in it.

Seeing this, a rousing cheer broke from the crowd of people, who tossed their hats and waved their handkerchiefs and hailed the Scarecrow as their King. The soldiers joined the people in the cheering, for now they fully realized that their hated master was conquered and it would be wise to show their good will to the conqueror. Some of them bound Krewl with ropes and dragged him forward, dumping his body on the ground before the Scarecrow's throne. Googly-Goo struggled until he finally slid off the limb of the tree and came tumbling to the ground.

He then tried to sneak away and escape, but the soldiers seized and bound him beside Krewl.

"The tables are turned," said the Scarecrow, swelling out his chest until the straw within it crackled pleasantly, for he was highly pleased; "but it was you and your people who did it, friend Ork, and from this time you may count me your humble servant."

## CHAPTER 19

# The Conquest of the Witch

Now as soon as the conquest of King Krewl had taken place, one of the Orks had been dispatched to Pon's house with the joyful news. At once Gloria and Pon and Trot and Button-Bright hastened toward the castle. They were somewhat surprised by the sight that met their eyes, for there was the Scarecrow, crowned King, and all the people kneeling humbly before him. So they likewise bowed low to the new ruler and then stood beside the throne. Cap'n Bill, as the gray grasshopper, was still perched upon Trot's shoulder, but now he hopped to the shoulder of the Scarecrow and whispered into the painted ear:

"I thought Gloria was to be Queen of Jinxland." The Scarecrow shook his head.

"Not yet," he answered. "No Queen with a frozen heart is fit to rule any country." Then he turned to his new friend, the Ork, who was strutting about, very proud of what he had done, and said: "Do you suppose you, or your followers, could find old Blinkie the Witch?"

"Where is she?" asked the Ork.

"Somewhere in Jinxland, I'm sure."

"Then," said the Ork, "we shall certainly be able to find her."

"It will give me great pleasure," declared the Scarecrow. "When you have found her, bring her here to me. and I will then decide what to do with her."

The Ork called his followers together and spoke a few words to them in a low tone. A moment after they rose into the air — so suddenly that the Scarecrow, who was very light in weight, was blown quite out of his throne and into the arms of Pon, who replaced him carefully upon his seat. There was an eddy of dust and ashes, too, and the grasshopper only saved himself from being whirled into the crowd of people by jumping into a tree, from where a series of hops soon brought him back to Trot's shoulder again.

The Orks were quite out of sight by this time, so the Scarecrow made a speech to the people and presented Gloria to them, whom they knew well already and were fond of. But not all of them knew of her frozen heart, and when the Scarecrow related the story of the Wicked Witch's misdeeds, which had been encouraged and paid for by Krewl and Googly-Goo, the people were very indignant.

Meantime the fifty Orks had scattered all over Jinxland, which is not a very big country, and their sharp eyes were peering into every valley and grove and gully. Finally one of them spied a pair of heels sticking out from underneath some bushes, and with a shrill whistle to warn his comrades that the witch was found the Ork flew down and dragged old Blinkie from her hiding-place. Then two or three of the Orks seized the clothing of the wicked woman in their strong claws and, lifting her high in the air, where she struggled and screamed to no avail, they flew with her straight to the royal castle and set her down before the throne of the Scarecrow.

"Good!" exclaimed the straw man, nodding his stuffed head with satisfaction. "Now we can proceed to business. Mistress Witch, I am obliged to request,

gently but firmly, that you undo all the wrongs you have done by means of your witchcraft."

"Pah!" cried old Blinkie in a scornful voice. "I defy you all! By my magic powers I can turn you all into pigs, rooting in the mud, and I'll do it if you are not careful."

"I think you are mistaken about that," said the Scarecrow, and rising from his throne he walked with wobbling steps to the side of the Wicked Witch. "Before I left the Land of Oz, Glinda the Royal Sorceress gave me a box, which I was not to open except in an emergency. But I feel pretty sure that this occasion is an emergency; don't you, Trot?" he asked, turning toward the little girl.

"Why, we've got to do *something*," replied Trot seriously. . "Things seem in an awful muddle here, jus' now, and they'll be worse if we don't stop this witch from doing more harm to people."

"That is my idea, exactly," said the Scarecrow, and taking a small box from his pocket he opened the cover and tossed the contents toward Blinkie.

The old woman shrank back, pale and trembling, as a fine white dust settled all about her. Under its influence she seemed to the eyes of all observers to shrivel and grow smaller.

# Chapter Nineteen

"Oh, dear — oh, dear!" she wailed, wringing her hands in fear. "Haven't you the antidote, Scarecrow? Didn't the great Sorceress give you another box?"

"She did," answered the Scarecrow.

"Then give it me — quick!" pleaded the witch. "Give it me — and I'll do anything you ask me to!"

"You will do what I ask first," declared the Scarecrow, firmly.

The witch was shriveling and growing smaller every moment.

"Be quick, then!" she cried. "Tell me what I must do and let me do it, or it will be too late."

"You made Trot's friend, Cap'n Bill, a grasshopper. I command you to give him back his proper form again," said the Scarecrow.

"Where is he? Where's the grasshopper? Quick — quick!" she screamed.

Cap'n Bill, who had been deeply interested in this conversation, gave a great leap from Trot's shoulder and landed on that of the Scarecrow. Blinkie saw him alight and at once began to make magic passes and to mumble magic incantations. She was in a desperate hurry, knowing that she had no time to waste, and the grasshopper was so suddenly transformed into the old sailor-man, Cap'n Bill, that he had no opportunity to jump off the Scarecrow's shoulder; so his great weight bore the stuffed Scarecrow to the ground. No harm was done, however, and the straw man got up and brushed the dust from his clothes while Trot delightedly embraced Cap'n Bill.

"The other box! Quick! Give me the other box," begged Blinkie, who had now shrunk to half her former size.

"Not yet," said the Scarecrow. "You must first melt Princess Gloria's frozen heart."

"I can't; it's an awful job to do that! I can't," asserted the witch, in an agony of fear — for still she was growing smaller.

"You must!" declared the Scarecrow, firmly.

The witch cast a shrewd look at him and saw that he meant it; so she began dancing around Gloria in a frantic manner. The Princess looked coldly on, as if not at all interested in the proceedings, while Blinkie tore a handful of hair from her own head and ripped a strip of cloth from the bottom of her gown. Then the witch sank upon her knees, took a purple powder from her black bag and sprinkled it over the hair and cloth.

"I hate to do it — I hate to do it!" she wailed,

"for there is no more of this magic compound in all the world. But I must sacrifice it to save my own life. A match! Give me a match, quick!" and panting from lack of breath she gazed imploringly from one to another.

Cap'n Bill was the only one who had a match, but he lost no time in handing it to Blinkie, who quickly set fire to the hair and the cloth and the purple powder. At once a purple cloud enveloped Gloria, and this gradually turned to a rosy pink color — brilliant and quite transparent. Through the rosy

cloud they could all see the beautiful Princess, standing proud and erect. Then her heart became visible, at first frosted with ice but slowly growing brighter and warmer until all the frost had disappeared and it was beating as softly and regularly as any other heart. And now the cloud dispersed and disclosed Gloria, her face suffused with joy, smiling tenderly upon the friends who were grouped about her.

Poor Pon stepped forward — timidly, fearing a repulse, but with pleading eyes and arms fondly outstretched toward his former sweetheart — and the Princess saw him and her sweet face lighted with a radiant smile. Without an instant's hesitation she threw herself into Pon's arms and this reunion of two loving hearts was so affecting that the people turned away and lowered their eyes so as not to mar the sacred joy of the faithful lovers.

But Blinkie's small voice was shouting to the Scarecrow for help.

"The antidote!" she screamed. "Give me the other box — quick!"

The Scarecrow looked at the witch with his quaint, painted eyes and saw that she was now no taller than his knee. So he took from his pocket the second box and scattered its contents on Blinkie. She ceased to

grow any smaller, but she could never regain her former size, and this the wicked old woman well knew.

She did not know, however, that the second powder had destroyed all her power to work magic, and seeking to be revenged upon the Scarecrow and his friends she at once began to mumble a charm so terrible in its effect that it would have destroyed half the population of Jinxland — had it worked. But it did not work at all, to the amazement of old Blinkie. And by this time the Scarecrow noticed what the little witch was trying to do, and said to her:

" Go home, Blinkie, and behave yourself. You are no longer a witch, but an ordinary old woman, and since you are powerless to do more evil I advise you to try to do some good in the world. Believe me, it is more fun to accomplish a good act than an evil one, as you will discover when once you have tried it."

But Blinkie was at that moment filled with grief and chagrin at losing her magic powers. She started away toward her home, sobbing and bewailing her fate, and not one who saw her go was at all sorry for her.

## CHAPTER 20

# Queen Gloria

Next morning the Scarecrow called upon all the courtiers and the people to assemble in the throne room of the castle, where there was room enough for all that were able to attend. They found the straw man seated upon the velvet cushions of the throne, with the King's glittering crown still upon his stuffed head. On one side of the throne, in a lower chair, sat Gloria, looking radiantly beautiful and fresh as a new-blown rose. On the other side sat Pon, the gardener's boy, still dressed in his old smock frock and looking sad and solemn; for Pon could not make himself believe that so splendid a Princess would condescend to love him when she had come to her own and was seated upon a throne. Trot and Cap'n Bill sat at the feet of the Scarecrow and were much interested in the proceedings. Button-Bright had lost himself before breakfast, but came into the throne room before the ceremonies were over. Back of the throne stood a row of the great Orks, with their leader in the center, and the entrance to the palace was guarded by more Orks, who were regarded with wonder and awe.

When all were assembled, the Scarecrow stood up and made a speech. He told how Gloria's father, the good King Kynd, who had once ruled them and been loved by everyone, had been destroyed by King Phearce, the father of Pon, and how King Phearce had been destroyed by King Krewl. This last King had been a bad ruler, as they knew very well, and the Scarecrow declared that the only one in all Jinxland who had the right to sit upon the throne was Princess Gloria, the daughter of King Kynd.

"But," he added, "it is not for me, a stranger, to say who shall rule you. You must decide for yourselves, or you will not be content. So choose now who shall be your future ruler."

And they all shouted: "The Scarecrow! The Scarecrow shall rule us!"

# Chapter Twenty

Which proved that the stuffed man had made himself very popular by his conquest of King Krewl, and the people thought they would like him for their King. But the Scarecrow shook his head so vigorously that it became loose, and Trot had to pin it firmly to his body again.

"No," said he, "I belong in the Land of Oz, where I am the humble servant of the lovely girl who rules us all — the royal Ozma. You must choose one of your own inhabitants to rule over Jinxland. Who shall it be?"

They hesitated for a moment, and some few cried: "Pon!" but many more shouted: "Gloria!"

So the Scarecrow took Gloria's hand and led her to the throne, where he first seated her and then took the glittering crown off his own head and placed it upon that of the young lady, where it nestled prettily amongst her soft curls. The people cheered and shouted then, kneeling before their new Queen; but Gloria leaned down and took Pon's hand in both her own and raised him to the seat beside her.

"You shall have both a King and a Queen to care for you and to protect you, my dear subjects," she said in a sweet voice, while her face glowed with happiness; "for Pon was a King's son before he became a gardener's boy, and because I love him he is to be my Royal Consort."

That pleased them all, especially Pon, who realized that this was the most important moment of his life. Trot and Button-Bright and Cap'n Bill all congratulated him on winning the beautiful Gloria; but the Ork sneezed twice and said that in his opinion the young lady might have done better.

Then the Scarecrow ordered the guards to bring in the wicked Krewl, King no longer, and when he appeared, loaded with chains and dressed in fustian, the people hissed him and drew back as he passed so their garments would not touch him.

Krewl was not haughty or overbearing any more; on the contrary he seemed very meek and in great fear of the fate his conquerors had in store for him. But Gloria and Pon were too happy to be revengeful and so they offered to appoint Krewl to the position of gardener's boy at the castle, Pon having resigned to become King. But they said he must promise to reform his wicked ways and to do his duty faithfully, and he must change his name from Krewl to Grewl. All this the man eagerly promised to do, and so when Pon retired to a room in the castle to put on princely raiment, the old brown smock he had formerly worn was given to Grewl, who then went out into the garden to water the roses.

The remainder of that famous day, which was long remembered in Jinxland, was given over to feasting and merrymaking. In the evening there was a grand

dance in the courtyard, where the brass band played a new piece of music called the " Ork Trot " which was dedicated to " Our Glorious Gloria, the Queen."

While the Queen and Pon were leading this dance, and all the Jinxland people were having a good time, the strangers were gathered in a group in the park outside the castle. Cap'n Bill, Trot, Button-Bright and the Scarecrow were there, and so was their old friend the Ork; but of all the great flock of Orks which had assisted in the conquest but three remained in Jinxland, besides their leader, the others having returned to their own country as soon as Gloria was crowned Queen. To the young Ork who had accompanied them in their adventures Cap'n Bill said:

"You've surely been a friend in need, and we're mighty grateful to you for helping us. I might have been a grasshopper yet if it hadn't been for you, an' I might remark that bein' a grasshopper isn't much fun."

"If it hadn't been for you, friend Ork," said the Scarecrow, "I fear I could not have conquered King Krewl."

"No," agreed Trot, "you'd have been just a heap of ashes by this time."

"And I might have been lost yet," added Button-Bright. "Much obliged, Mr. Ork."

"Oh, that's all right," replied the Ork. "Friends must stand together, you know, or they wouldn't be friends. But now I must leave you and be off to my own country, where there's going to be a surprise party on my uncle, and I've promised to attend it."

# Chapter Twenty

"Dear me," said the Scarecrow, regretfully. "That is very unfortunate."

"Why so?" asked the Ork.

"I hoped you would consent to carry us over those mountains, into the Land of Oz. My mission here is now finished and I want to get back to the Emerald City."

"How did you cross the mountains before?" inquired the Ork.

"I scaled the cliffs by means of a rope, and crossed the Great Gulf on a strand of spider web. Of course I can return in the same manner, but it would be a hard journey — and perhaps an impossible one — for Trot and Button-Bright and Cap'n Bill. So I thought that if you had the time you and your people would carry us over the mountains and land us all safely on the other side, in the Land of Oz."

The Ork thoughtfully considered the matter for a while. Then he said:

"I mustn't break my promise to be present at the surprise party; but, tell me, could you go to Oz to-night?"

"What, now?" exclaimed Trot.

"It is a fine moonlight night," said the Ork, "and I've found in my experience that there's no time so good as right away. The fact is," he explained, "it's a long journey to Orkland and I and my cousins here are all rather tired by our day's work. But if you will start now, and be content to allow us to carry you over the mountains and dump you on the other side, just say the word and — off we go!"

Cap'n Bill and Trot looked at one another questioningly. The little girl was eager to visit the famous fairyland of Oz and the old sailor had endured such hardships in Jinxland that he would be glad to be out of it.

"It's rather impolite of us not to say good-bye to the new King and Queen," remarked the Scarecrow, "but I'm sure they're too happy to miss us, and I assure you it will be much easier to fly on the backs of the Orks over those steep mountains than to climb them as I did."

"All right; let's go!" Trot decided. "But where's Button-Bright?"

Just at this important moment Button-Bright was lost again, and they all scattered in search of him. He had been standing beside them just a few minutes before, but his friends had an exciting hunt for him before they finally discovered the boy seated among the members of the band, beating the end of the bass drum with the bone of a turkey-leg that he had taken from the table in the banquet room.

"Hello, Trot," he said, looking up at the little girl when she found him. "This is the first chance I ever had to pound a drum with a reg'lar drum stick. And I ate all the meat off the bone myself."

"Come quick. We're going to the Land of Oz."

"Oh, what's the hurry?" said Button-Bright; but she seized his arm and dragged him away to the park, where the others were waiting.

Trot climbed upon the back of her old friend, the Ork leader, and the others took their seats on the backs of his three cousins. As soon as all were placed and clinging to the skinny necks of the creatures, the revolving tails began to whirl and up rose the four monster Orks and sailed away toward the mountains. They were so high in the air that when they passed the crest of the highest peak it seemed far below them. No sooner were they well across the barrier than the Orks swooped downward and landed their passengers upon the ground.

"Here we are, safe in the Land of Oz!" cried the Scarecrow joyfully.

"Oh, are we?" asked Trot, looking around her curiously.

She could see the shadows of stately trees and the outlines of rolling hills; beneath her feet was soft turf, but otherwise the subdued light of the moon disclosed nothing clearly.

"Seems jus' like any other country," was Cap'n Bill's comment.

"But it isn't," the Scarecrow assured him. "You

are now within the borders of the most glorious fairy-land in all the world. This part of it is just a corner of the Quadling Country, and the least interesting portion of it. It's not very thickly settled, around here, I'll admit, but — "

He was interrupted by a sudden whir and a rush of air as the four Orks mounted into the sky.

" Good night! " called the shrill voices of the strange creatures, and although Trot shouted " Good night! "

as loudly as she could, the little girl was almost ready to cry because the Orks had not waited to be properly thanked for all their kindness to her and to Cap'n Bill.

But the Orks were gone, and thanks for good deeds do not amount to much except to prove one's politeness.

"Well, friends," said the Scarecrow, "we mustn't stay here in the meadows all night, so let us find a pleasant place to sleep. Not that it matters to me, in the least, for I never sleep; but I know that meat people like to shut their eyes and lie still during the dark hours."

"I'm pretty tired," admitted Trot, yawning as she followed the straw man along a tiny path, "so, if you don't find a house handy, Cap'n Bill and I will sleep under the trees, or even on this soft grass."

But a house was not very far off, although when the Scarecrow stumbled upon it there was no light in it whatever. Cap'n Bill knocked on the door several times, and there being no response the Scarecrow boldly lifted the latch and walked in, followed by the others. And no sooner had they entered than a soft light filled the room. Trot couldn't tell where it came from, for no lamp of any sort was visible, but she did not waste much time on this problem, because directly in the center of the room stood a table set for three, with lots of good food on it and several of the dishes smoking hot.

The little girl and Button-Bright both uttered exclamations of pleasure, but they looked in vain for any cook stove or fireplace, or for any person who might have prepared for them this delicious feast.

"It's fairyland," muttered the boy, tossing his cap in a corner and seating himself at the table. "This supper smells 'most as good as that turkey-leg I had in Jinxland. Please pass the muffins, Cap'n Bill."

Trot thought it was strange that no people but themselves were in the house, but on the wall opposite the door was a gold frame bearing in big letters the word:

"WELCOME."

So she had no further hesitation in eating of the food so mysteriously prepared for them.

"But there are only places for three!" she exclaimed.

"Three are quite enough," said the Scarecrow. "I never eat, because I am stuffed full already, and I like my nice clean straw better than I do food."

# The Scarecrow of Oz

Trot and the sailor-man were hungry and made a hearty meal, for not since they had left home had they tasted such good food. It was surprising that Button-Bright could eat so soon after his feast in Jinxland, but the boy always ate whenever there was an opportunity. "If I don't eat now," he said, "the next time I'm hungry I'll wish I had."

"Really, Cap'n," remarked Trot, when she found a dish of ice-cream appear beside her plate, "I b'lieve this is fairyland, sure enough."

"There's no doubt of it, Trot," he answered gravely.

"I've been here before," said Button-Bright, "so I know."

After supper they discovered three tiny bedrooms adjoining the big living room of the house, and in each room was a comfortable white bed with downy pillows. You may be sure that the tired mortals were not long in bidding the Scarecrow good night and creeping into their beds, where they slept soundly until morning.

For the first time since they set eyes on the terrible whirlpool, Trot and Cap'n Bill were free from anxiety and care. Button-Bright never worried about anything. The Scarecrow, not being able to sleep, looked out of the window and tried to count the stars.

## CHAPTER 21

# Dorothy, Betsy and Ozma

I suppose many of my readers have read descriptions of the beautiful and magnificent Emerald City of Oz, so I need not describe it here, except to state that never has any city in any fairyland ever equalled this one in stately splendor. It lies almost exactly in the center of the Land of Oz, and in the center of the Emerald City rises the wall of glistening emeralds that surrounds the palace of Ozma. The palace is almost a city in itself and is inhabited by many of the Ruler's especial friends and those who have won her confidence and favor.

As for Ozma herself, there are no words in any

dictionary I can find that are fitted to describe this young girl's beauty of mind and person. Merely to see her is to love her for her charming face and manners; to know her is to love her for her tender sympathy, her generous nature, her truth and honor. Born of a long line of Fairy Queens, Ozma is as nearly perfect as any fairy may be, and she is noted for her wisdom as well as for her other qualities. Her happy subjects adore their girl Ruler and each one considers her a comrade and protector.

At the time of which I write, Ozma's best friend and most constant companion was a little Kansas girl named Dorothy, a mortal who had come to the Land of Oz in a very curious manner and had been offered a home in Ozma's palace. Furthermore, Dorothy had been made a Princess of Oz, and was as much at home in the royal palace as was the gentle Ruler. She knew almost every part of the great country and almost all of its numerous inhabitants. Next to Ozma she was loved better than anyone in all Oz, for Dorothy was simple and sweet, seldom became angry and had such a friendly, chummy way that she made friends whereever she wandered. It was she who first brought the Scarecrow and the Tin Woodman and the Cowardly Lion to the Emerald City. Dorothy had also introduced to Ozma the Shaggy Man and the Hungry Tiger, as well as Billina the Yellow Hen, Eureka the Pink Kitten, and many other delightful characters and creatures. Coming as she did from our world, Dorothy was much like many other girls we know; so there were times when she was not so wise as she might have been, and other times when she was obstinate and got herself into trouble. But life in a fairyland had taught the little girl to accept all sorts of surprising things as matters-of-course, for while Dorothy was no fairy — but just as mortal as we are — she had seen more wonders than most mortals ever do.

Another little girl from our outside world also lived in Ozma's palace. This was Betsy Bobbin, whose strange adventures had brought her to the Emerald City, where Ozma had cordially welcomed her. Betsy was a shy little thing and could never get used to the marvels that surrounded her, but she and Dorothy were firm friends and thought themselves very fortunate in being together in this delightful country.

One day Dorothy and Betsy were visiting Ozma in the girl Ruler's private apartment, and among the things that especially interested them was Ozma's Magic Picture, set in a handsome frame and hung upon the wall of the room. This picture was a magic one because it constantly changed its scenes and showed events and adventures happening in all parts of the world. Thus it was really a "moving picture" of life, and if the one who stood before it wished to know what any absent person was doing, the picture instantly showed that person, with his or her surroundings.

The two girls were not wishing to see anyone in particular, on this occasion, but merely enjoyed watching the shifting scenes, some of which were exceedingly curious and remarkable. Suddenly Dorothy exclaimed: "Why, there's Button-Bright!" and this drew Ozma also to look at the picture, for she and Dorothy knew the boy well.

"Who is Button-Bright?" asked Betsy, who had never met him.

"Why, he's the little boy who is just getting off the back of that strange flying creature," exclaimed Dorothy. Then she turned to Ozma and asked: "What is that thing, Ozma? A bird? I've never seen anything like it before."

"It is an Ork," answered Ozma, for they were watching the scene where the Ork and the three big birds were first landing their passengers in Jinxland.

after the long flight across the desert. "I wonder," added the girl Ruler, musingly, " why those strangers dare venture into that unfortunate country, which is ruled by a wicked King."

"That girl, and the one-legged man, seem to be mortals from the outside world," said Dorothy.

"The man isn't one-legged," corrected Betsy; "he has one wooden leg."

"It's almost as bad," declared Dorothy, watching Cap'n Bill stump around.

"They are three mortal adventurers," said Ozma, "and they seem worthy and honest. But I fear they will be treated badly in Jinxland, and if they meet with any misfortune there it will reflect upon me, for Jinxland is a part of my dominions."

"Can't we help them in any way?" inquired Dorothy. "That seems like a nice little girl. I'd be sorry if anything happened to her."

"Let us watch the picture for awhile," suggested Ozma, and so they all drew chairs before the Magic Picture and followed the adventures of Trot and Cap'n Bill and Button-Bright. Presently the scene shifted and showed their friend the Scarecrow crossing the mountains into Jinxland, and that somewhat relieved Ozma's anxiety, for she knew at once that

Glinda the Good had sent the Scarecrow to protect the strangers.

The adventures in Jinxland proved very interesting to the three girls in Ozma's palace, who during the succeeding days spent much of their time in watching the picture. It was like a story to them.

"That girl's a reg'lar trump!" exclaimed Dorothy, referring to Trot, and Ozma answered:

Dorothy

" She's a dear little thing, and I'm sure nothing very bad will happen to her. The old sailor is a fine character, too, for he has never once grumbled over being a grasshopper, as so many would have done."

When the Scarecrow was so nearly burned up the girls all shivered a little, and they clapped their hands in joy when the flock of Orks came and saved him.

So it was that when all the exciting adventures in Jinxland were over and the four Orks had begun their flight across the mountains to carry the mortals into the Land of Oz, Ozma called the Wizard to her and asked him to prepare a place for the strangers to sleep.

The famous Wizard of Oz was a quaint little man who inhabited the royal palace and attended to all the magical things that Ozma wanted done. He was not as powerful as Glinda, to be sure, but he could do a great many wonderful things. He proved this by placing a house in the uninhabited part of the Quadling Country where the Orks landed Cap'n Bill and Trot and Button-Bright, and fitting it with all the comforts I have described in the last chapter.

Next morning Dorothy said to Ozma:

" Oughtn't we to go meet the strangers, so we can show them the way to the Emerald City? I'm sure that little girl will feel shy in this beautiful land, and I know if 'twas me I'd like somebody to give me a welcome."

Ozma smiled at her little friend and answered:

"You and Betsy may go to meet them, if you wish, but I can not leave my palace just now, as I am to have a conference with Jack Pumpkinhead and Professor Wogglebug on important matters. You may take the Sawhorse and the Red Wagon, and if you start soon you will be able to meet the Scarecrow and the strangers at Glinda's palace."

"Oh, thank you!" cried Dorothy, and went away to tell Betsy and to make preparations for the journey.

## CHAPTER 22

# The Waterfall

Glinda's castle was a long way from the mountains, but the Scarecrow began the journey cheerfully, since time was of no great importance in the Land of Oz and he had recently made the trip and knew the way. It never mattered much to Button-Bright where he was or what he was doing; the boy was content in being alive and having good companions to share his wanderings. As for Trot and Cap'n Bill, they now found themselves so comfortable and free from danger, in this fine fairyland, and they were so awed and amazed by the adventures they were encountering, that the journey to Glinda's castle was more like a

# Chapter Twenty-Two

pleasure trip than a hardship, so many wonderful things were there to see.

Button-Bright had been in Oz before, but never in this part of it, so the Scarecrow was the only one who knew the paths and could lead them. They had eaten a hearty breakfast, which they found already prepared for them and awaiting them on the table when they arose from their refreshing sleep, so they left the magic house in a contented mood and with hearts lighter and more happy than they had known for many a day. As they marched along through the fields, the sun shone brightly and the breeze was laden with delicious fragrance, for it carried with it the breath of millions of wildflowers.

At noon, when they stopped to rest by the banks of a pretty river, Trot said with a long-drawn breath that was much like a sigh:

"I wish we'd brought with us some of the food that was left from our breakfast, for I'm getting hungry again."

Scarcely had she spoken when a table rose up before them, as if from the ground itself, and it was loaded with fruits and nuts and cakes and many other good things to eat. The little girl's eyes opened wide at this display of magic, and Cap'n Bill was not sure that the things were actually there and fit to eat until he had taken them in his hand and tasted them. But the Scarecrow said with a laugh:

"Someone is looking after your welfare, that is certain, and from the looks of this table I suspect my friend the Wizard has taken us in his charge. I've known him to do things like this before, and if we are in the Wizard's care you need not worry about your future."

"Who's worrying?" inquired Button-Bright, already at the table and busily eating.

The Scarecrow looked around the place while the others were feasting, and finding many things unfamiliar to him he shook his head and remarked:

"I must have taken the wrong path, back in that last valley, for on my way to Jinxland I remember that I passed around the foot of this river, where there was a great waterfall."

"Did the river make a bend, after the waterfall?" asked Cap'n Bill.

"No, the river disappeared. Only a pool of whirling water showed what had become of the river; but I suppose it is under ground, somewhere, and will come to the surface again in another part of the country."

"Well," suggested Trot, as she finished her luncheon, "as there is no way to cross this river, I s'pose we'll have to find that waterfall, and go around it."

"Exactly," replied the Scarecrow; so they soon renewed their journey, following the river for a long time until the roar of the waterfall sounded in their ears. By and by they came to the waterfall itself, a sheet of silver dropping far, far down into a tiny lake which seemed to have no outlet. From the top of the fall, where they stood, the banks gradually sloped away, so that the descent by land was quite easy, while the river could do nothing but glide over an edge of rock and tumble straight down to the depths below.

"You see," said the Scarecrow, leaning over the brink, "this is called by our Oz people the Great Waterfall, because it is certainly the highest one in all the land; but I think — Help!"

He had lost his balance and pitched headforemost into the river. They saw a flash of straw and blue clothes, and the painted face looking upward in surprise. The next moment the Scarecrow was swept over the waterfall and plunged into the basin below.

The accident had happened so suddenly that for a moment they were all too horrified to speak or move.

"Quick! We must go to help him or he will be drowned," Trot exclaimed.

Even while speaking she began to descend the bank to the pool below, and Cap'n Bill followed as swiftly as his wooden leg would let him. Button-Bright came more slowly, calling to the girl:

"He can't drown, Trot; he's a Scarecrow."

But she wasn't sure a Scarecrow couldn't drown and never relaxed her speed until she stood on the edge of the pool, with the spray dashing in her face. Cap'n Bill, puffing and panting, had just voice enough to ask, as he reached her side:

"See him, Trot?"

"Not a speck of him. Oh, Cap'n, what do you s'pose has become of him?"

"I s'pose," replied the sailor, "that he's in that water, more or less far down, and I'm 'fraid it'll make his straw pretty soggy. But as fer his bein' drowned, I agree with Button-Bright that it can't be done."

There was small comfort in this assurance and Trot stood for some time searching with her eyes the bubbling water, in the hope that the Scarecrow would finally come to the surface. Presently she heard Button-Bright calling: "Come here, Trot!" and looking around she saw that the boy had crept over the

wet rocks to the edge of the waterfall and seemed to be peering behind it. Making her way toward him, she asked:

"What do you see?"

"A cave," he answered. "Let's go in. P'r'aps we'll find the Scarecrow there."

She was a little doubtful of that, but the cave interested her, and so did it Cap'n Bill. There was just space enough at the edge of the sheet of water for them to crowd in behind it, but after that dangerous entrance they found room enough to walk upright and after a time they came to an opening in the wall of rock. Approaching this opening, they gazed within it and found a series of steps, cut so that they might easily descend into the cavern.

Trot turned to look inquiringly at her companions. The falling water made such din and roaring that her voice could not be heard. Cap'n Bill nodded his head, but before he could enter the cave, Button-Bright was before him, clambering down the steps without a particle of fear. So the others followed the boy.

The first steps were wet with spray, and slippery, but the remainder were quite dry. A rosy light seemed to come from the interior of the cave, and this lighted their way. After the steps there was a short tunnel, high enough for them to walk erect in. and then they reached the cave itself and paused in wonder and admiration.

They stood on the edge of a vast cavern, the walls and domed roof of which were lined with countless rubies, exquisitely cut and flashing sparkling rays from one to another. This caused a radiant light that permitted the entire cavern to be distinctly seen, and the effect was so marvelous that Trot drew in her breath with a sort of a gasp, and stood quite still in wonder.

But the walls and roof of the cavern were merely a setting for a more wonderful scene. In the center was a bubbling caldron of water, for here the river rose again, splashing and dashing till its spray rose high in the air, where it took the ruby color of the jewels and seemed like a seething mass of flame. And while they gazed into the tumbling, tossing water, the body of the Scarecrow suddenly rose in the center, struggling and kicking, and the next instant wholly disappeared from view.

"My, but he's wet!" exclaimed Button-Bright; but none of the others heard him.

Trot and Cap'n Bill discovered that a broad ledge — covered, like the walls, with glittering rubies —

ran all around the cavern; so they followed this gorgeous path to the rear and found where the water made its final dive underground, before it disappeared entirely. Where it plunged into this dim abyss the river was black and dreary looking, and they stood gazing in awe until just beside them the body of the Scarecrow again popped up from the water.

## CHAPTER 23

# The Land of Oz

The straw man's appearance on the water was so sudden that it startled Trot, but Cap'n Bill had the presence of mind to stick his wooden leg out over the water and the Scarecrow made a desperate clutch and grabbed the leg with both hands. He managed to hold on until Trot and Button-Bright knelt down and seized his clothing, but the children would have been powerless to drag the soaked Scarecrow ashore had not Cap'n Bill now assisted them. When they laid him on the ledge of rubies he was the most useless looking Scarecrow you can imagine — his straw sodden and dripping with water, his clothing wet and crumpled, while even the sack upon which his face was painted had become so wrinkled that the old jolly expression of their stuffed friend's features was entirely gone. But he could still speak, and when Trot bent down her ear she heard him say:

"Get me out of here as soon as you can."

That seemed a wise thing to do, so Cap'n Bill lifted his head and shoulders, and Trot and Button-Bright each took a leg; among them they partly carried and partly dragged the damp Scarecrow out of the Ruby Cavern, along the tunnel, and up the flight of rock steps. It was somewhat difficult to get him past the edge of the waterfall, but they succeeded, after much effort, and a few minutes later laid their poor comrade on a grassy bank where the sun shone upon him freely and he was beyond the reach of the spray.

Cap'n Bill now knelt down and examined the straw that the Scarecrow was stuffed with.

"I don't believe it'll be of much use to him, any more," said he, "for it's full of polliwogs an' fish eggs, an' the water has took all the crinkle out o' the straw an' ruined it. I guess, Trot, that the best thing for us to do is to empty out all his body an' carry his head an' clothes along the road till we come to a field or a house where we can get some fresh straw."

# Chapter Twenty-Three

"Yes, Cap'n," she agreed, "there's nothing else to be done. But how shall we ever find the road to Glinda's palace, without the Scarecrow to guide us?"

"That's easy," said the Scarecrow, speaking in a rather feeble but distinct voice. "If Cap'n Bill will carry my head on his shoulders, eyes front, I can tell him which way to go."

So they followed that plan and emptied all the old, wet straw out of the Scarecrow's body. Then the sailor-man wrung out the clothes and laid them in the sun till they were quite dry. Trot took charge of the head and pressed the wrinkles out of the face as it dried, so that after a while the Scarecrow's expression became natural again, and as jolly as before.

This work consumed some time, but when it was completed they again started upon their journey, Button-Bright carrying the boots and hat, Trot the bundle of clothes, and Cap'n Bill the head. The Scarecrow, having regained his composure and being now in a good humor, despite his recent mishaps, beguiled their way with stories of the Land of Oz.

It was not until the next morning, however, that they found straw with which to restuff the Scarecrow. That evening they came to the same little house they had slept in before, only now it was magically transferred to a new place. The same bountiful supper as before was found smoking hot upon the table and the same cosy beds were ready for them to sleep in.

They rose early and after breakfast went out of doors, and there, lying just beside the house, was a heap of clean, crisp straw. Ozma had noticed the Scarecrow's accident in her Magic Picture and had notified the Wizard to provide the straw, for she knew the adventurers were not likely to find straw in the country through which they were now traveling.

They lost no time in stuffing the Scarecrow anew, and he was greatly delighted at being able to walk around again and to assume the leadership of the little party.

"Really," said Trot, "I think you're better than you were before, for you are fresh and sweet all through and rustle beautifully when you move."

"Thank you, my dear," he replied gratefully. "I always feel like a new man when I'm freshly stuffed. No one likes to get musty, you know, and even good straw may be spoiled by age."

"It was water that spoiled you, the last time," remarked Button-Bright, "which proves that too much bathing is as bad as too little. But, after all, Scarecrow, water is not as dangerous for you as fire."

# Chapter Twenty-Three

"All things are good in moderation," declared the Scarecrow. "But now, let us hurry on, or we shall not reach Glinda's palace by nightfall."

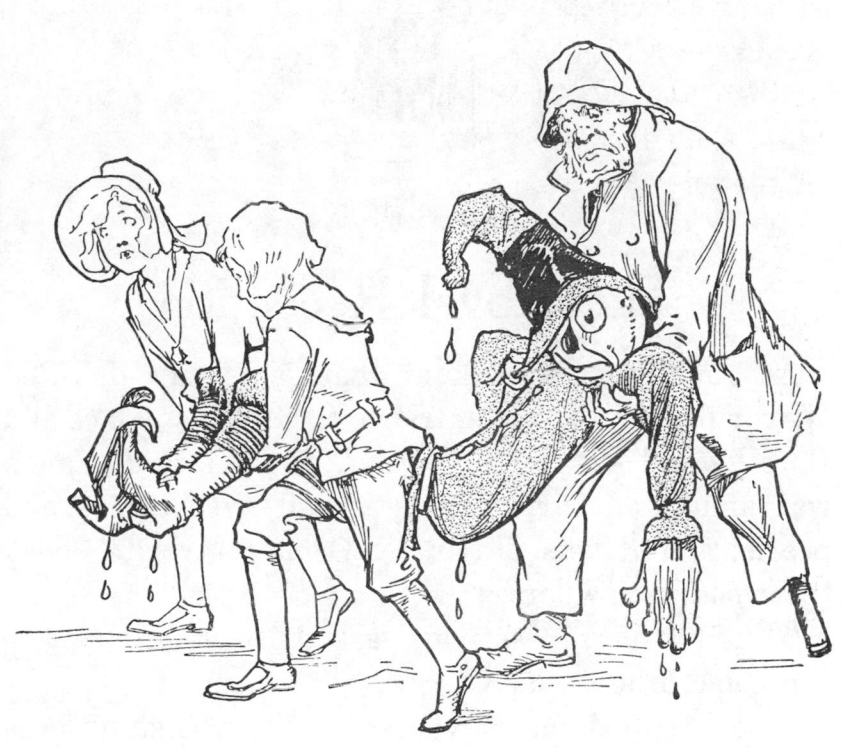

## CHAPTER 24

# The Royal Reception

At about four o'clock of that same day the Red Wagon drew up at the entrance to Glinda's palace and Dorothy and Betsy jumped out. Ozma's Red Wagon was almost a chariot, being inlaid with rubies and pearls, and it was drawn by Ozma's favorite steed, the wooden Sawhorse.

"Shall I unharness you," asked Dorothy, "so you can come in and visit?"

"No," replied the Sawhorse. "I'll just stand here and think. Take your time. Thinking doesn't seem to bore me at all."

"What will you think of?" inquired Betsy.

"Of the acorn that grew the tree from which I was made."

So they left the wooden animal and went in to see Glinda, who welcomed the little girls in her most cordial manner.

"I knew you were on your way," said the good Sorceress when they were seated in her library, "for I learned from my Record Book that you intended to meet Trot and Button-Bright on their arrival here."

"Is the strange little girl named Trot?" asked Dorothy.

"Yes; and her companion, the old sailor, is named Cap'n Bill. I think we shall like them very much, for they are just the kind of people to enjoy and appreciate our fairyland and I do not see any way, at present, for them to return again to the outside world."

"Well, there's room enough here for them, I'm sure," said Dorothy. "Betsy and I are already eager to welcome Trot. It will keep us busy for a year, at least, showing her all the wonderful things in Oz."

Glinda smiled.

"I have lived here many years," said she, "and I have not seen all the wonders of Oz yet."

Meantime the travelers were drawing near to the

palace, and when they first caught sight of its towers Trot realized that it was far more grand and imposing than was the King's castle in Jinxland. The nearer they came, the more beautiful the palace appeared, and when finally the Scarecrow led them up the great marble steps, even Button-Bright was filled with awe.

"I don't see any soldiers to guard the place," said the little girl.

"There is no need to guard Glinda's palace," replied the Scarecrow. "We have no wicked people in Oz, that we know of, and even if there were any, Glinda's magic would be powerful enough to protect her."

Button-Bright was now standing on the top steps of the entrance, and he suddenly exclaimed:

"Why, there's the Sawhorse and the Red Wagon! Hip, hooray!" and next moment he was rushing down to throw his arms around the neck of the wooden horse, which good-naturedly permitted this familiarity when it recognized in the boy an old friend.

Button-Bright's shout had been heard inside the palace, so now Dorothy and Betsy came running out to embrace their beloved friend, the Scarecrow, and to welcome Trot and Cap'n Bill to the Land of Oz.

"We've been watching you for a long time, in Ozma's Magic Picture," said Dorothy, "and Ozma has sent us to invite you to her own palace in the Em'rald City. I don't know if you realize how lucky you are to get that invitation, but you'll understand it better after you've seen the royal palace and the Em'rald City."

Glinda now appeared in person to lead all the party into her Azure Reception Room. Trot was a little afraid of the stately Sorceress, but gained courage by holding fast to the hands of Betsy and Dorothy. Cap'n Bill had no one to help him feel at ease, so the old sailor sat stiffly on the edge of his chair and said: " Yes, ma'am," or " No, ma'am," when he was spoken to, and was greatly embarrassed by so much splendor.

The Scarecrow had lived so much in palaces that he felt quite at home, and he chatted to Glinda and the Oz girls in a merry, light-hearted way. He told all about his adventures in Jinxland, and at the Great Waterfall, and on the journey hither — most of which his hearers knew already — and then he asked Dorothy and Betsy what had happened in the Emerald City since he had left there.

They all passed the evening and the night at Glinda's palace, and the Sorceress was so gracious to Cap'n Bill that the old man by degrees regained his self-possession and began to enjoy himself. Trot had already come to the conclusion that in Dorothy and Betsy she had found two delightful comrades, and Button-Bright was just as much at home here as he had been in the fields of Jinxland or when he was buried in the popcorn snow of the Land of Mo.

The next morning they arose bright and early and after breakfast bade good-bye to the kind Sorceress, whom Trot and Cap'n Bill thanked earnestly for sending the Scarecrow to Jinxland to rescue them. Then they all climbed into the Red Wagon.

There was room for all on the broad seats, and when all had taken their places — Dorothy, Trot and Betsy on the rear seat and Cap'n Bill, Button-Bright and the Scarecrow in front — they called "Gid-dap!" to the Sawhorse and the wooden steed moved briskly away, pulling the Red Wagon with ease.

It was now that the strangers began to perceive the real beauties of the Land of Oz, for they were passing through a more thickly settled part of the country and the population grew more dense as they drew nearer to the Emerald City. Everyone they met had a cheery word or a smile for the Scarecrow, Dorothy and Betsy Bobbin, and some of them remembered Button-Bright and welcomed him back to their country.

# Chapter Twenty-Four

It was a happy party, indeed, that journeyed in the Red Wagon to the Emerald City, and Trot already began to hope that Ozma would permit her and Cap'n Bill to live always in the Land of Oz.

When they reached the great city they were more amazed than ever, both by the concourse of people in their quaint and picturesque costumes, and by the splendor of the city itself. But the magnificence of the Royal Palace quite took their breath away, until Ozma received them in her own pretty apartment and by her charming manners and assuring smiles made them feel they were no longer strangers.

Trot was given a lovely little room next to that of Dorothy, while Cap'n Bill had the cosiest sort of a room next to Trot's and overlooking the gardens. And that evening Ozma gave a grand banquet and reception in honor of the new arrivals. While Trot had read of many of the people she then met, Cap'n Bill was less familiar with them and many of the unusual characters introduced to him that evening caused the old sailor to open his eyes wide in astonishment.

He had thought the live Scarecrow about as curious as anyone could be, but now he met the Tin Woodman, who was all made of tin, even to his heart, and carried

# RUDE HAND GESTURES OF THE WORLD

**A GUIDE TO OFFENDING WITHOUT WORDS**

*by* **Romana Lefevre**
*photographs by* **Daniel Castro**

**CHRONICLE BOOKS**

SAN FRANCISCO

Library of Congress Cataloging-in-Publication Data available.

ISBN: 978-0-8118-7807-4

Manufactured in China

Typeset by Suzanne M. LaGasa

10 9 8

Chronicle Books LLC
680 Second Street
San Francisco, California 94107
www.chroniclebooks.com

# TABLE OF CONTENTS

# INTRODUCTION

Evolutionary anthropologists tell us that gesture is much older than speech. When early humans had something to say, they said it with their hands. And because manners didn't come along until a great deal later, it seems safe to assume that much of what people said was rude. Perhaps they wanted to disparage Og's performance in the bison hunt or the size of Bog's manhood. We don't know what signs they used, but we can be sure they used some.

By the time history was being recorded, its rude hand gestures were, too. Many of these are still in use today. Ancients insulted one another using many of the same gestures we use now, often with surprising gusto and frequency. In ancient Rome, the gesture popularly known as the Finger was so common that it even had a name: *digitus impudicus.*

Over the next several thousand years, the language of hand gesture continued to evolve, with each region of the world developing its own colorful vocabulary of rude signs. These gestures express not just vulgar sentiments but deep truths about the culture itself. The insults a given culture favors are very revealing. Just as the Eskimos have many words for "snow," so the French have an infinite number of gestures to express ennui; the Lebanese, romantic desires; and the British, an urgent wish that you "piss off."

The language of hand signals continues to grow and change, with new gestures entering the vocabulary all the time. New gesturers enter as well. For most of history, hand gesturing—even the non-vulgar variety—was an almost exclusively male activity. Happily, in much of the world, that is no longer true, as more and more women proudly give the Bird.

Hand gestures point, quite literally, to where we've been and where we're going. They are especially relevant today. The advent of air travel means that one can find oneself in a distant country in a matter of hours and knowing not a single word. We hope this book will make your travels easier—and much more interesting.

It is easy for an innocent abroad to commit an unforgivable faux pas. Learn the gestures that follow, and you will be innocent no more; your missteps will be made with purpose and intent. Let the offending begin!

# BUSINESS AND

## NEGOTIATIONS

When doing business abroad, it is important to know the local body language. The uninformed can easily commit terrible blunders without even knowing what they've done. Every culture is different, and what is considered polite in one office environment can be deeply offensive in another. In Japan, for instance, one causes affront by presenting a business card using one hand instead of two. Crossing one's legs in Saudi Arabia, especially if this exposes the sole of the shoe, is a grievous insult. Knowing the local customs will ensure you don't accidentally give offense.

At other times, however, giving offense is exactly what the savvy businessperson must do. Perhaps you want to communicate your distrust or to inform your associates they're being stingy. To avoid being taken advantage of, you must let the dishonest know you're on to them. When negotiations get tough, these gestures will help you maintain the upper hand.

# FISHY SMELL

**Meaning:** I find you untrustworthy.
**Used in:** Southern Italy

In business, it is important to let your associates know you can't be taken advantage of. This gesture informs them you are on to their attempts to deceive. To perform, move your nose side to side with the index and middle finger. The movement suggests that something stinks, and you are trying to rid yourself of the odor.

*"I find you untrustworthy."*

# CRAB HANDS

**Meaning:** Not to be trusted
**Used in:** Southern Italy

Although crabs themselves are perfectly honest and straight-forward, it is true that their manner of walking—an unpredictable, side-to-side scamper—suggests otherwise. This hand gesture, another southern Italian accusation of deceit, links the pinky fingers to mimic a crab's movements, implying that the subject is untrustworthy.

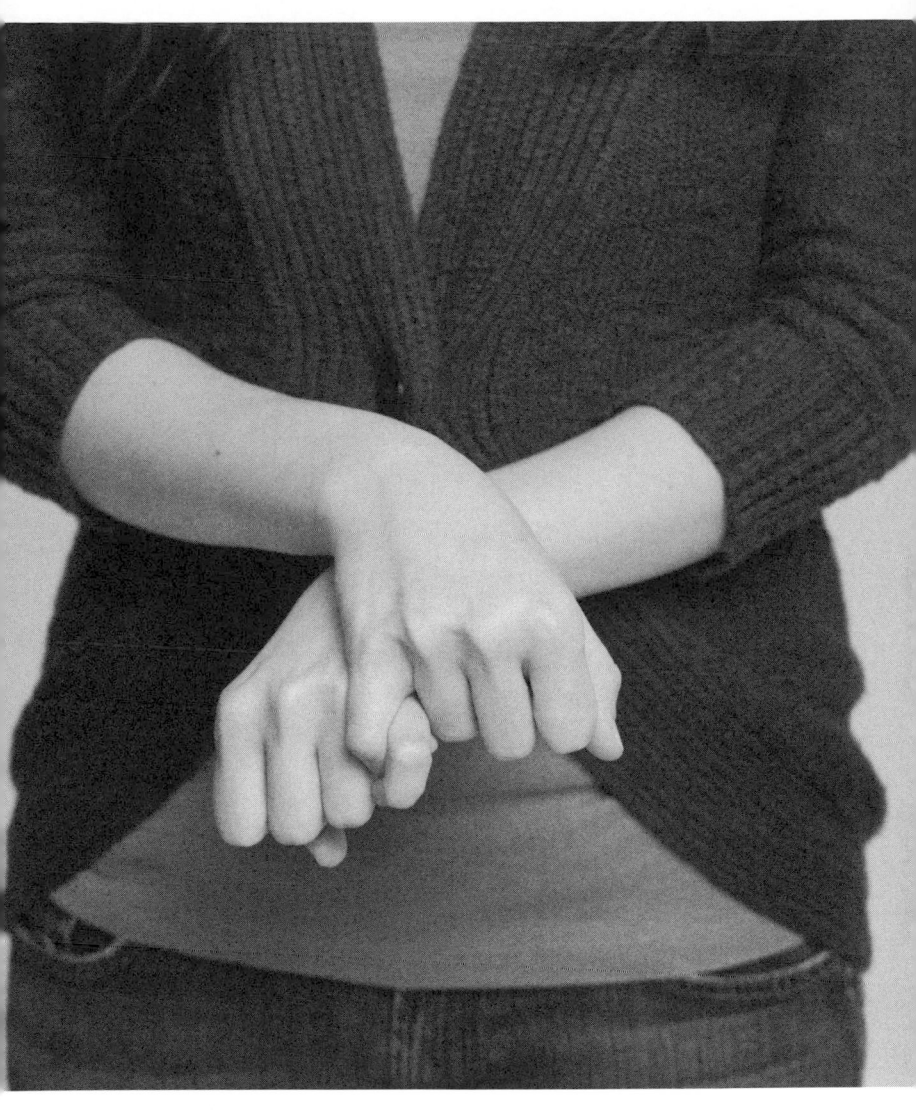

*"He is not to be trusted."*

# PAPO FURADO

**Meaning:** Bullshit
**Used in:** Brazil

*Papo furado* is a Brazilian idiom that means "prattle," "trivial chit-chat," or, more frankly, "bullshit." To make the accompanying gesture, place a flat, extended hand under the chin. This gesture, which should be performed only behind the back of the subject, lets the others in the room know that his idle talk should be disregarded.

**NOTE:** In other parts of the Americas and western Europe, this gesture means "fed up." The chin should be tapped several times to underscore your exasperation.

*"That's bullshit."*

# TACAÑO

**Meaning:** You're stingy.
**Used in:** Mexico, South America

Just as the heart is associated with love, so, in many Latin American countries, is the elbow with stinginess. In Mexico the two are so closely linked that a miser is described as *muy codo* (very elbow), the idea being that he rarely straightens it to pay the check. If your *compadre* makes a habit of failing to pick up the check, you may wish to correct his behavior with this sharp gesture. For extra emphasis, bang your elbow on the table.

**NOTE:** In Austria and Germany the same gesture means "You're an idiot," suggesting that the elbow is where the subject keeps his brain.

*"You're stingy."*

17

# STICKY FINGERS

**Meaning:** Thief
**Used in:** South America

It is an unfortunate fact that, from time to time, we must encounter people who will try to steal what is ours. When this happens in South America, you may bring it to others' attention with this gesture. Simply sweep your arm across the table as if trying to gather any money that might be there. Of course, if you actually gather some money while doing this, your companions will soon be making this gesture in reference to you.

**NOTE:** In Peru, this gesture more frequently means "money." In other South American countries, it can mean "pay up."

*"He's a thief."*

# GRASS IN HAND

**Meaning:** You are deluded.
**Used in:** Israel

As any visitor to Israel knows, the local population is not shy about conveying their feelings openly and honestly. With this gesture, one conveys the feeling that the subject is openly and honestly full of it. The index finger points at the upturned palm of the other hand to imply that "grass will grow on my hand before what you say comes true."

*"You are deluded."*

# ROMANCE AND
# INTIMATE RELATIONS

In your travels, a continental sophisticate like yourself is likely to encounter individuals with whom you share a spark—but not a language. How to indicate to the young lady that you would like to get to know her better? How to inform the mysterious stranger that his overtures are welcome? With the international language of gesture.

The hand gestures that follow will allow you to express your affections and are useful even if you are fluent in the local language. Even the smoothest operator can get tongue-tied before a beautiful young thing. Better to indicate your interest with a simple tap or a subtle flick.

Should the subtle gesture go unreciprocated, we also offer some more direct ones. These will not go unnoticed and are only to be used when you are fairly certain that they will be well received, as they may otherwise result in embarrassment, awkwardness, or an aggressive reprimand.

You will note that the great majority of these gestures are native to the Middle East, particularly Lebanon. It is not entirely clear why the Lebanese became the experts in this particular linguistic specialty. Perhaps its Arabian nights inspire ardor; perhaps an admirable native modesty requires that such negotiations take place silently. What is apparent is that the Lebanese dialect of sign language is a particularly romantic one.

# RENDEZVOUS FINGERS

**Meaning:** Romantic rendezvous
**Used in:** Egypt, North Africa

In many countries, tapping the index fingers together simply means that two individuals are meeting, but in parts of North Africa, it implies they are meeting for a very special purpose: the purpose of physical love. Though often used to comment on the relationships of others, in some regions, especially Egypt, it is viewed as an invitation to intercourse. Use with care, lest you receive an RSVP you weren't expecting.

*"That's a romantic rendezvous."*

# NECK RUB

**Meaning:** Romantic interest
**Used in:** Lebanon

Due, perhaps, to its exquisite sensitivity, the neck is considered one of the body's prime locations for romantic maneuvers. In America, "necking" is synonymous with the exchange of kisses. And in Lebanon, a man can indicate his romantic interest in a young lady simply by rubbing the back of his own neck. Those prone to a stiff neck should be careful about tending to it in public, lest their attempt to work out a crick attract too many paramours.

*"I feel a romantic interest."*

# NOSE BRUSH

**Meaning:** Romantic interest
**Used in:** Jordan

There are many different ways to invite a young lady to the boudoir. One might send roses, compose a sonnet, or beseech her from her balcony. And all this is charming, this dance of love, but it can be inefficient and slow. Happily, in Jordan, there is a shortcut. Would-be Romeos may signal their interest to potential Juliets by brushing the forefinger across the bridge of the nose. Would an invitation by any other method smell as sweet?

*"I desire a romantic exchange."*

# HIT THAT

**Meaning:** Shall we have sex?
**Used in:** Middle East

Should Rendezvous Fingers, the Neck Rub, and the Nose Brush fail, you may want to try this more obvious gesture to invite a young lady to bed. Make a fist with one hand and then repeatedly punch the open palm of the other. The blows should mimic the rhythm of the act of love, like a romantic metronome. If it succeeds, you'll soon be making sweet music together.

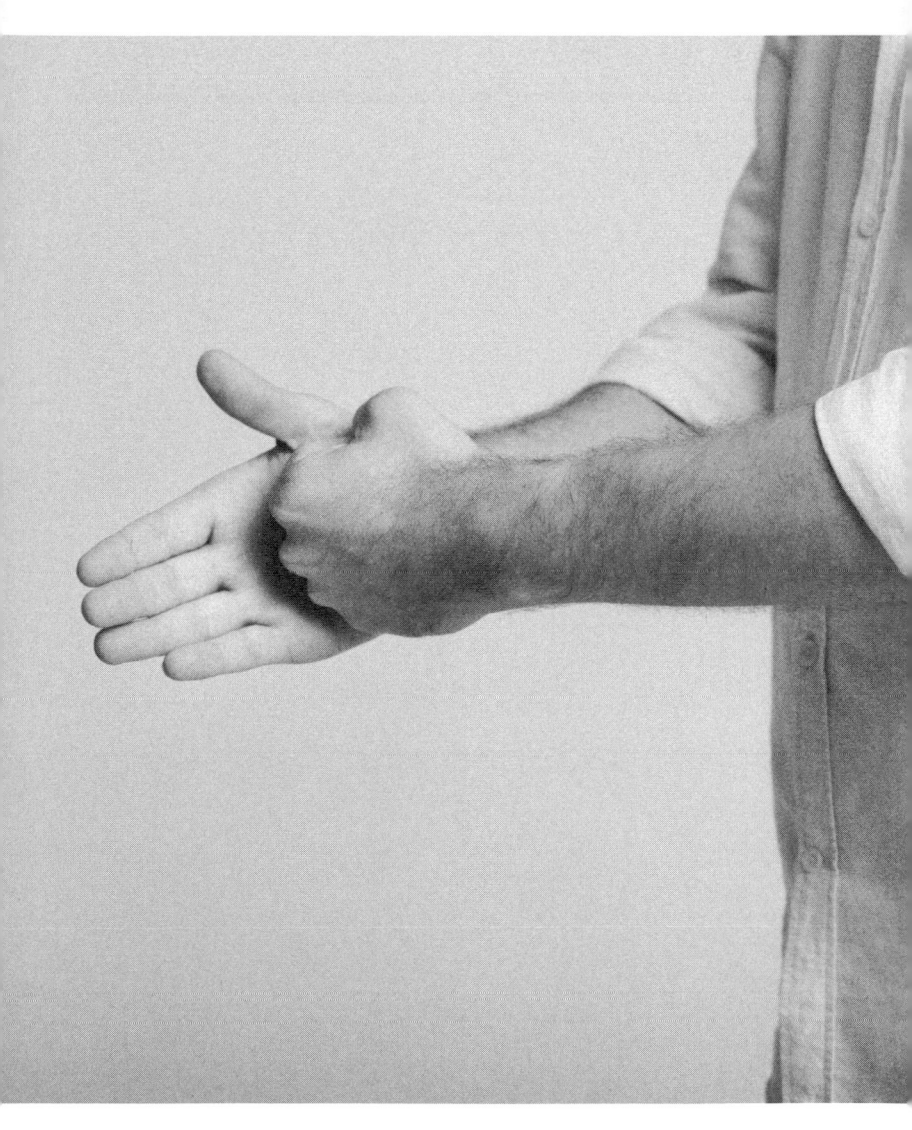

*"Shall we have sex?"*

# PALMS

**Meaning:** Copulation
**Used in:** Lebanon

In this gesture, the back of the left hand is ground into the palm of the right in a rather artless pantomime of copulation. It is used to describe the sex act but not to initiate it. Vulgar and crude, it serves as a poor invitation to lovemaking, unless the invitee is vulgar and crude as well.

*"They are copulating."*

# HIGH BEAMS

**Meaning:** I would like to caress her breasts.
**Used in:** Lebanon and Syria

Yet another Middle Eastern expression of desire, this one indicates that the gesturer would like to caress the bosom of a certain woman. To perform, hold the hand horizontally and rotate as though screwing in a lightbulb. Use with care. When executed inappropriately, it is unlikely you'll be screwing anything at all.

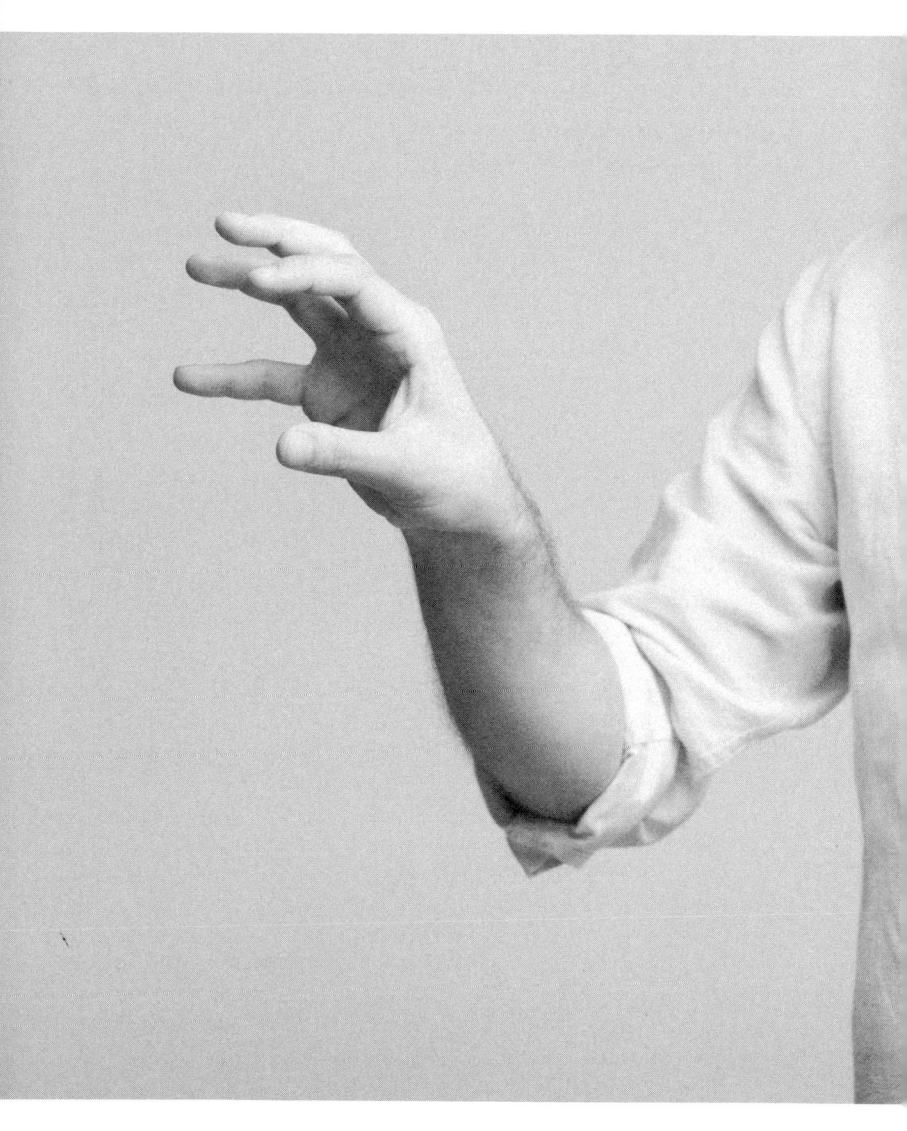

*"I would like to caress her breasts."*

# V ON THE NOSE

**Meaning:** Sexual intercourse
**Used in:** Middle East, Central America, South America

In this gesture, the face is a canvas for a tableau about the act of love, in which the fingers represent the lady's parts, and the nose, the gentleman's. Lewd and rude, its use should be confined to locker room talk. The result is an insulting work of art sure to generate controversy and conversation.

*"They are engaging in sexual intercourse."*

# HAND INTERCOURSE

**Meaning:** Sexual intercourse
**Used in:** Worldwide

Perhaps the crudest and most obvious of hand gestures, this sign is simple, effective, and highly offensive. With one hand representing the phallus and the other the female flower, the fingers are brought together rhythmically in a gesture that is lost on no one. Low on wit and subtlety but high on clarity, this gesture should be used when blatancy and directness are your goal.

*"Let's screw."*

# BIRD IN HAND

**Meaning:** Homosexual
**Used in:** Lebanon, Libya, Saudi Arabia

One of several Middle Eastern gestures that indicate homosexuality, this one is made by pursing the fingers and the thumb together to resemble a pecking bird. The disparaging suggestion is that homosexuals are birdlike in their gestures and that the subject is a bird of that feather.

**NOTE:** Hand signals tend toward the rude and offensive, and while gay rights have advanced in much of the world, the language of hand gesture remains, unfortunately, rather homophobic. There are many signs for homosexuality, more of them derogatory. These include:

–Making a horizontal OK gesture (Middle East, Mediterranean)

–Holding the hand out flat, palm down, and rotating from side to side (Colombia)

–Circling the nose with the thumb and forefinger (North America)

–Licking the little finger, then smoothing the eyebrow (worldwide)

*"He's a homosexual."*

# SAPPHIC PALM RUB

**Meaning:** Lesbian
**Used in:** South America

While there are scores of hand gestures indicating the homo-sexuality of a man, this is one of the very few that indicate the homosexuality of a woman. The gesturer rubs both palms together in such a manner that suggests sexual contact without penetration. Though not always derogatory, it is crude and overly forward. A variant of the gesture repeatedly slaps palms together as if making tortillas (*tortillera*, or tortilla maker, is slang for lesbian in some South and Central American countries, a somewhat disparaging reference to the masculine upper arm strength tortilla makers acquire).

*"She's a lesbian."*

# EVASIVE MANEUVERS

When traveling internationally, you may meet many people you would like to know better—and a few you hope never to see again. If you don't speak the language, it can be difficult to communicate this sentiment politely and even more difficult to communicate it rudely, as you sometimes must. The gestures in this chapter will help you make your wishes clear.

We also include them in part so that you will understand them when they are directed at you, particularly if you are traveling to France, for France is where the overwhelming majority of these gestures originated. This is just as it should be. After all, the French are devoted to the silent art form of mime; no wonder they should have thought up so many wordless gestures that ask you to stop talking and leave them alone. And as with all things French, these gestures are artful and elegant. *Très chic!*

# LES BOULES

**Meaning:** Exasperated
**Used in:** France

Should you find yourself losing your patience while in France, this gesture will express your frustration clearly and offensively. The literal translation is "to have the balls," and the accompanying gesture mimes the annoying balls one is burdened with. *Quelle dommage!*

*"I'm exasperated."*

# LA RÉPÈTE

**Meaning:** Displeasure
**Used in:** France

In this French hand signal, the gesturer cups an ear to feign deafness. This is not a request for you to repeat what you just said even more loudly but to stop speaking altogether. As the French say, "talk is silver, but silence is gold."

*"I'm displeased."*

# LE CAMEMBERT

**Meaning:** Shut up.
**Used in:** France

This gesture is as sharp and pungent as a fine French cheese. Also known as the *clapet* or the *ferme-la*, it is often accompanied by an exhortation to *ferme la bouche* ("shut your mouth") and mimics the closing of the mouth. To make the gesture, hold the fingers straight and then clamp them against the thumb, as if grasping a wedge of cheese.

*"Shut up."*

# CHIN FLICK

**Meaning:** Get lost.
**Used in:** Belgium, France, Northern Italy, Tunisia

In France, this gesture is known as *la barbe*, or "the beard," the idea being that the gesturer is flashing his masculinity in much the same way that a buck will brandish his horns or a cock his comb. Simply brush the hand under the chin in a forward flicking motion. While not as aggressive as flashing one's actual genitalia, this gesture is legal and remains effective as a mildly insulting brush-off.

**NOTE:** In Italy, this gesture simply means "No."

*"Get lost."*

# BARBED BRUSH

**Meaning:** I grow bored.
**Used in:** France

Another gesture that references *la barbe*—which in French can mean "boring" as well as "the beard"—this one has the gesturer stroke his cheek as if checking for facial hair. The implication is that the subject has been droning on so long that the listener has grown a full beard. To avoid this insult, visitors to France would do well to keep their conversations as short as their stubble.

*"I grow bored."*

# ON SE TIRE

**Meaning:** Get lost.
**Used in:** France, Belgium, Greece, Italy, Spain, Tunisia, Yugoslavia

In this gesture of dismissal, the left hand chops or clamps down on the right wrist, forcing the right hand to flick up. The chopping motion mimics the severing of a thief's hand and tells the subject he deserves to be banished like a common bandit. The gesture can also be used without insulting intent to signify "Let's go."

*"Get lost."*

# LA FLUTE

**Meaning:** I tire of your made-up nonsense.
**Used in:** France

Yet another French expression of impatience, this one requires the gesturer to play an imaginary flute. He thus connotes his weariness with the dubious story, suggesting that the subject's falsehood become as long-winded as an endless flute solo. Should you be on the receiving end of such a gesture, it is best to switch to another conversational key or silence your instrument altogether.

*"I tire of your made-up nonsense."*

# WRITE-OFF

**Meaning:** I am ignoring you.
**Used in:** Greece

The literal translation of *st'arxidia mou*, the phrase that accompanies this gesture, is "I write it on my testicles." And while there may well be people who, out of a strange psychological compulsion or simply boredom, actually write on their testicles, here the threat is simply metaphorical and tells the subject you're ignoring him. One needn't possess testicles to use the gesture, which is employed by men and women alike.

*"I am ignoring you."*

# DIPLOMACY

It is an unfortunate fact that there are stupid, lazy, and ugly people all over the world, and many of them are unaware of their own shortcomings. Ideally one would be able to keep such criticisms to oneself, but circumstances may dictate that you share your feelings. Perhaps you need to let your English student know his work is not up to par, or maybe you must suggest that your neighbor see a mental health professional. Perhaps you must tell your driver that he is lazy or your would-be Internet bride that she is less attractive than you were expecting. Sometimes difficult sentiments must be shared.

Whatever the message, it is important that it be conveyed diplomatically. The gestures in this chapter will let you share bad news, if not with sensitivity, at least with humor. Many may also be used playfully. They all will help you say what you can't say out loud.

# ESTÚPIDO

**Meaning:** You are very stupid.
**Used in:** South America

It is impolite to point out the stupidity of others, but sometimes it must be done. In parts of South America, it can be accomplished simply and directly by holding out the hand with the palm up and all fingers spread. The gesture is an expression of exasperation with the subject's hopeless incompetence. Even the biggest imbecile is sure to understand this message.

*"You are very stupid."*

# IDIOTA

**Meaning:** Are you an idiot?
**Used in:** Brazil

Another South American gesture indicating stupidity, this one requires improv skills and an actorly flair. To perform, put your fist to your forehead while making a comical overbite. The gesture is most effective when accented with multiple grunts of arrr, arrr. When executed correctly, you will be rewarded with appreciative laughs, though not, perhaps, from your subject.

*"Are you an idiot?"*

# STUPID HEAD

**Meaning:** You are stupid and/or crazy.
**Used in:** Japan

In Japan, stupidity is indicated by this gesture, in which you point an index finger at your temple and rotate the finger twice. If the subject's stupidity is insufficiently expressed by this maneuver, you may increase the insult by opening the hand abruptly and shouting "Pah!" The gesture can be used both seriously and in jest, so if offense is your intent, be sure to perform it aggressively. If even more aggression is required, consider slapping the subject on the back of the head while yelling *"Baka!"* ("You fool!").

*"You are stupid and crazy."*

# BUSU

**Meaning:** Ugly
**Used in:** Japan

If the subject is not just stupid but ugly, you may add insult to injury with this gesture. To execute the maneuver—which is used to comment on the unattractiveness of a woman—push the nose up with the index finger. This mimics the snout of a pig, which the Japanese find especially repulsive, as prominent nostrils are not considered attractive. In Japan, it is also considered somewhat repulsive to blow your nose in public. Should you do so, you may get to witness the Busu gesture for yourself.

*"You are ugly."*

# PEPPER MILL

**Meaning:** Crazy
**Used in:** Southern Italy

In southern Italy, craziness is indicated by this gesture, in which one mimics the grinding of a pepper mill. The implication is that the subject's addled brain is whirring as fast as the mill's blades.

*"You are crazy."*

# HUEVON

**Meaning:** What uncomfortably large testicles you have.
**Used in:** Latin America, Mexico

The medical term for enlarged testicles is orchitis, and it is a condition requiring medical attention. Here the suggestion is not that the subject may be ill, but that his oversized genitalia are making him lazy and, perhaps, rendering him undesirable to women. To make the gesture, which is used only between men, simply cup a palm upward, as if holding something heavy. Medical attention is not required, but an apology may be.

*"What uncomfortably large testicles you have."*

# QUEEN ANNE'S FAN

**Meaning:** Mockery
**Used in:** Worldwide

This very old gesture has a single meaning—mockery—but several dozen monikers. In England alone, it is known by sixteen different names, including "cocking a snook" (that is, making a snout) and Queen Anne's Fan, a reference to the sign language of fans that became popular during Queen Anne's reign in the eighteenth century. Its origins are unknown, but it is surmised that the gesture is meant to mimic a deformed nose or a cock's comb. The insult it delivers is mild and playful. For added whimsy, waggle the fingers or line up the second hand behind the first.

*"I mock you."*

# LEFT HAND

**Meaning:** I am touching you or your food with the hand
I just wiped myself with.
**Used in:** Islamic countries

While not a rude gesture per se, using one's left hand in any
Islamic country is a faux pas sure to cause offense and discomfort.
In these regions, the left hand is traditionally reserved for bodily
hygiene, and to offer food or a handshake with that hand is to
invite revulsion, not to mention fears of hepatitis. Limit use of your
left hand unless revulsion is your intent.

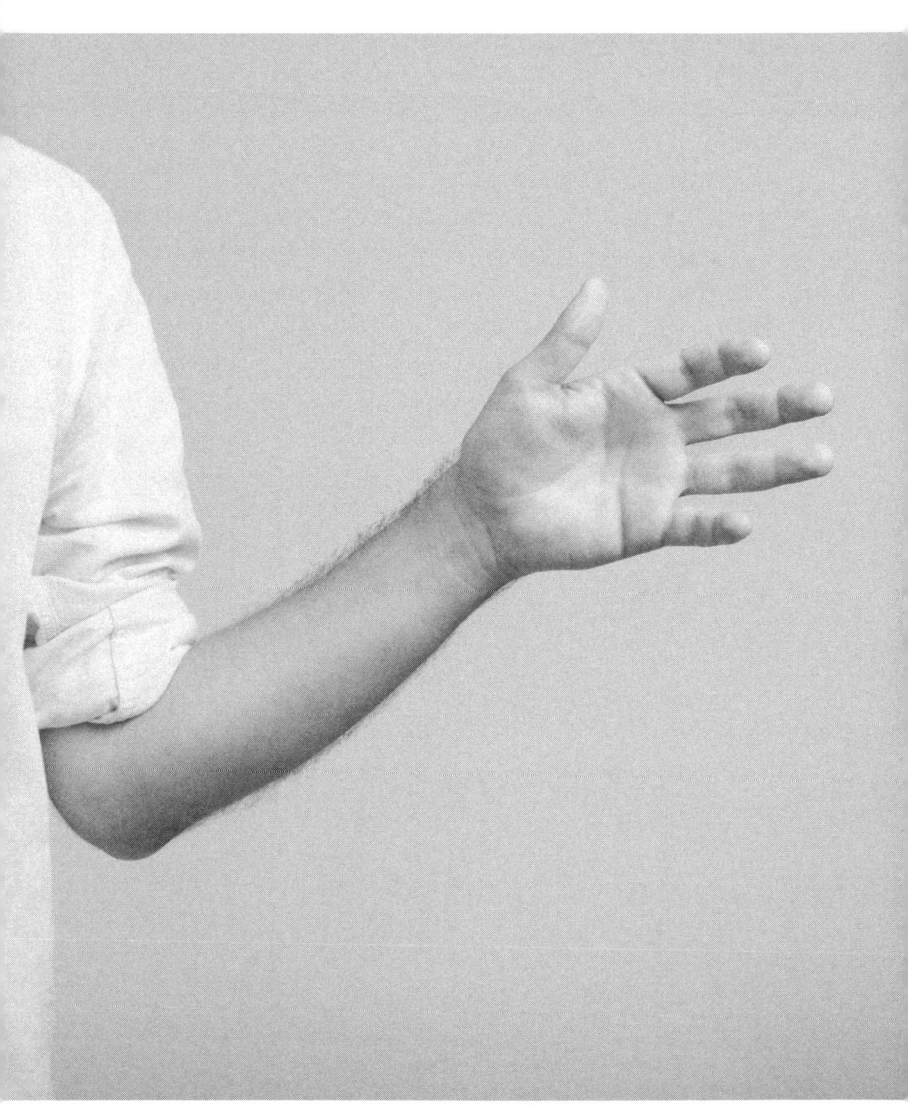

*"I am touching you or your food with the hand I just wiped myself with."*

# ADVANCED DIPLOMACY

Some messages can't be expressed through jokes or subtle hints. When you truly need to give insult, the kid gloves must be removed. Direct and forthright communication is required. The frank gestures in this chapter will express your point clearly, whether that point is that you'd like to rub excrement in the subject's face or that his mother is a prostitute.

Be warned that the gestures that follow are highly inflammatory. Some are illegal, some are ill advised, and all are incredibly offensive. Fisticuffs, destruction of property, and ejection from the premises are virtually guaranteed. Rioting is a distinct possibility. They are to be used only as a measure of last resort.

But as any adventurer knows, a last resort is sometimes necessary. When it's time to get your hands dirty, these filthy hand gestures will do the job.

# DONKEY RIDE

**Meaning:** I will ride you like a donkey.
**Used in:** Saudi Arabia

An elaborate two-handed gesture, this sign is like a puppet show in which the fingers act out an intricate maneuver whose message is "I will ride you like a donkey." To make the gesture, form an upside-down V (representing the rider's legs) with the first two fingers of your right hand and then straddle the left forefinger (representing the donkey). Orchestrating this gesture does not take much less effort than actually mounting the subject, but it is considerably less awkward.

*"I will ride you like a donkey."*

# FIVE FATHERS

**Meaning:** You have five fathers, i.e., your mother is a whore.
**Used in:** Arab countries, Caribbean

If you are looking to get yourself deported from Saudi Arabia—possibly amid a riot—you can do no better than the Five Fathers gesture. The most inflammatory hand gesture in the Arab world, this sign accuses the subject's mother of cavorting with every Tom, Dick, and Mustafa, implying that she had so many suitors that paternity is impossible to determine. To execute, point your left index finger at your right hand, while pursing all fingers of the right hand together. The insult is extreme and almost certain to provoke violence.

*"Your mother is a whore."*

# HERE, DOGGIE

**Meaning:** Come here, you lowly dog.
**Used in:** The Philippines

When beckoning a companion in the Philippines, be sure to point the hand down, moving the fingers in a sort of pawing motion. The upturned forefinger beckon is used only for dogs, and to use it on a person implies that you think he is one. This is a highly offensive maneuver and is taken very seriously, sometimes resulting in the gesturer's arrest. A dog may be man's best friend, but should you use it on your human best friend, your best friend he will be no longer.

*"Come here, you lowly dog."*

# MOUTZA

**Meaning:** To hell with you! / I rub shit in your face! / I'm going to violate your sister! / I'm going to violate your entire family, including your dog!
**Used in:** Greece, Africa, Pakistan

The Moutza is among the most complex of hand gestures, as elaborate and ancient as a Japanese tea ceremony. Perhaps the oldest offensive hand signal still in use, the Moutza originated in ancient Byzantium, where it was the custom for criminals to be chained to a donkey and displayed on the street. There, local townsfolk might add to their humiliation by rubbing dirt, feces, and ashes (*moutzos* in medieval Greek) into their faces.

Now that the advent of modern sewage systems and antismoking laws means that these materials are no longer readily available, the Moutza is a symbolic stand-in. In Greece, it is often accompanied by commands including *par'ta* ("take these") or *órse* ("there you go"). Over the years, the versatile Moutza has acquired more connotations, including a sexual one, in which the five extended fingers suggest the five sexual acts the gesturer would like to perform with the subject's willing sister.

The Moutza has many variations, each appropriate to its own occasion. See variations on the following pages.

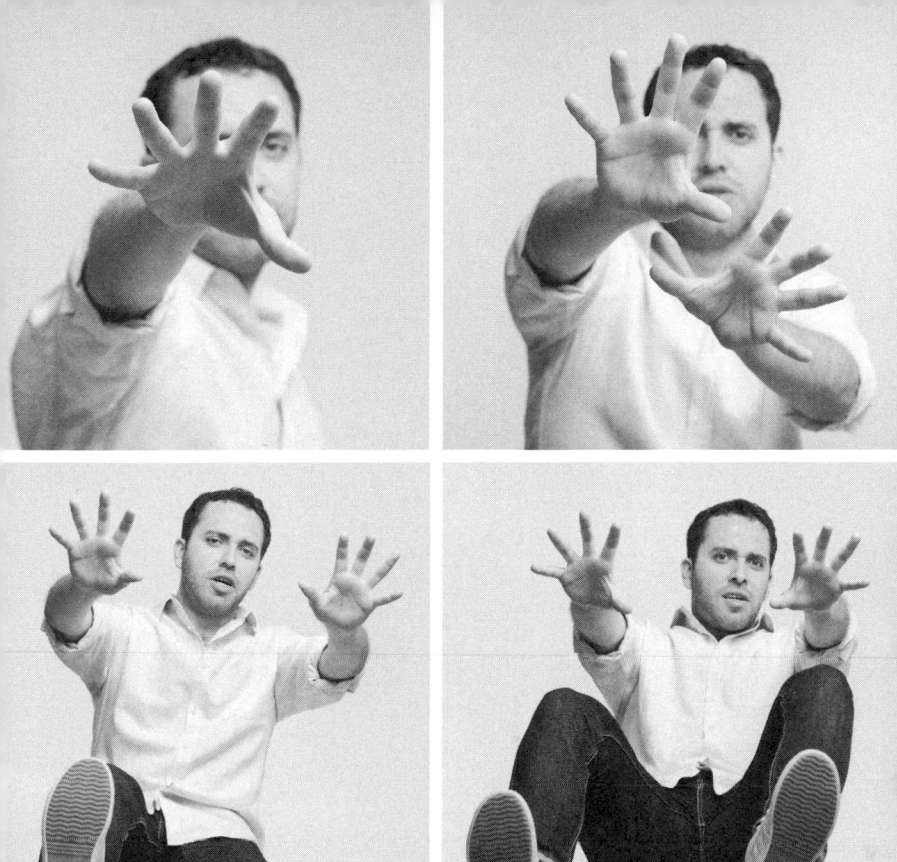

# CLASSIC MOUTZA

In the classic or full Moutza, all five fingers are extended at face level with the palm facing out. Appropriate times to use this gesture are when one is disrespected in traffic or when confronting an insolent service person.

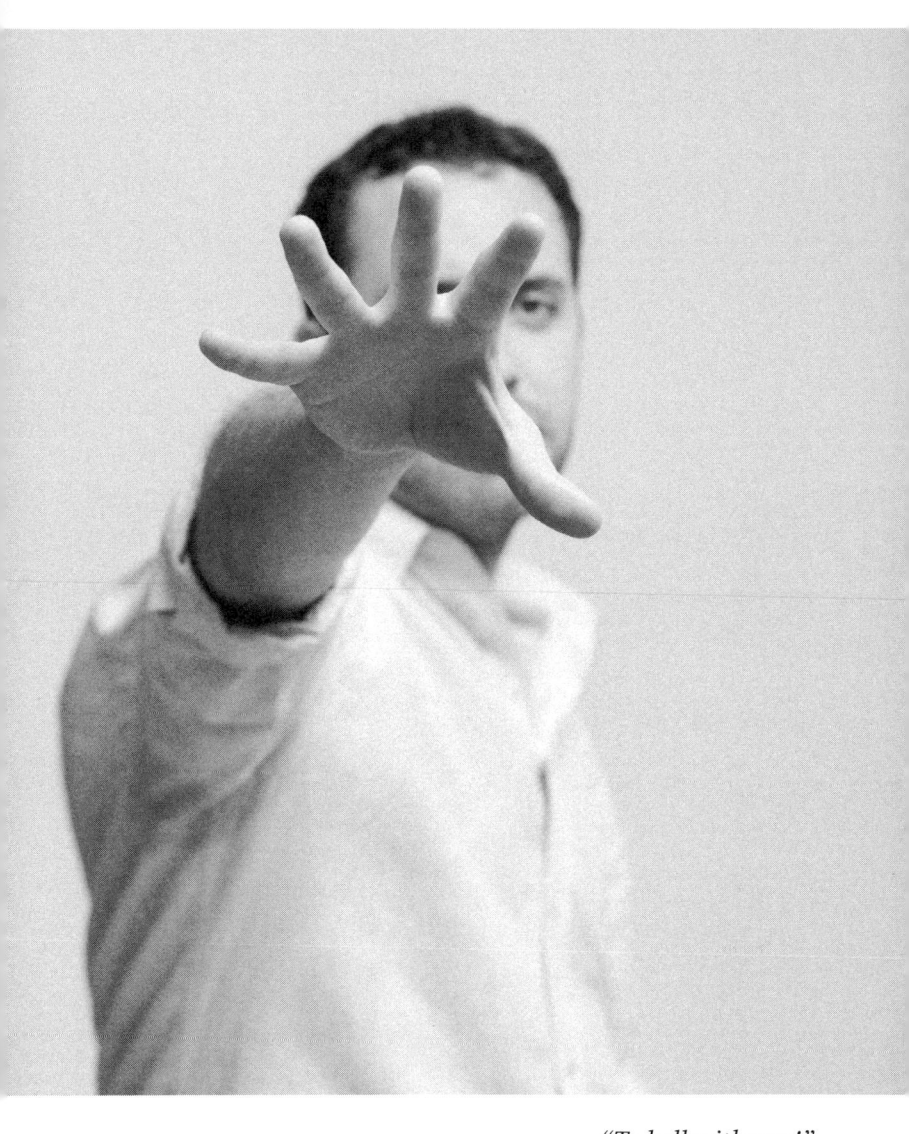

*"To hell with you!"*

# DOUBLE MOUTZA

When one wishes to express more ire than the classic Moutza permits, for example, as a prelude to a bar fight, the double Moutza is called for. In this variation, both hands assume the full Moutza position. The palm of one hand is then smacked against the back of the other. Perform this gesture as close as possible to the face of the subject to indicate extreme perturbation.

*"I rub shit in your face!"*

# TRIPLE MOUTZA

If double Moutza does not have the desired effect, the gesturer may proceed to triple Moutza. Position both hands in full Moutza; then extend a foot for three times the Moutza insult. Employ only when discovering one's spouse with one's best friend or on occasions when maximun provocation is desired.

*"I'm going to violate your sister!"*

# QUADRUPLE MOUTZA

To be used only in extreme cases, such as prison riots. The gesturer, who must be seated, extends both hands in full Moutza as well as both feet. The insult is severe and irremediable. Use only with strangers, as no existing relationship will survive such an affront.

*"I'm going to violate your entire family, including your dog!"*

# BEAST

**Meaning:** You're a beast.
**Used in:** Japan

This highly insulting gesture is unique to Japan. In execution, it is similar to the Moutza (page 88), but only four fingers are deployed, representing the four legs of an animal. The gesture references the oppressed *eta* (literally, "filthy mass") caste who were associated with four-legged animals due to their employment in slaughter-houses and leather workshops.

*"You're a beast."*

# WANKER

**Meaning:** Masturbation
**Used in:** North America, United Kingdom

In this coarse and explicit gesture, the hand is jerked repeatedly in a pantomime of male self-pleasure. The implication is that the subject is so hopeless that masturbation is his only recourse to sexual satisfaction. Its natural habitat is the football arena, where it is often employed by fans against the opposing team.

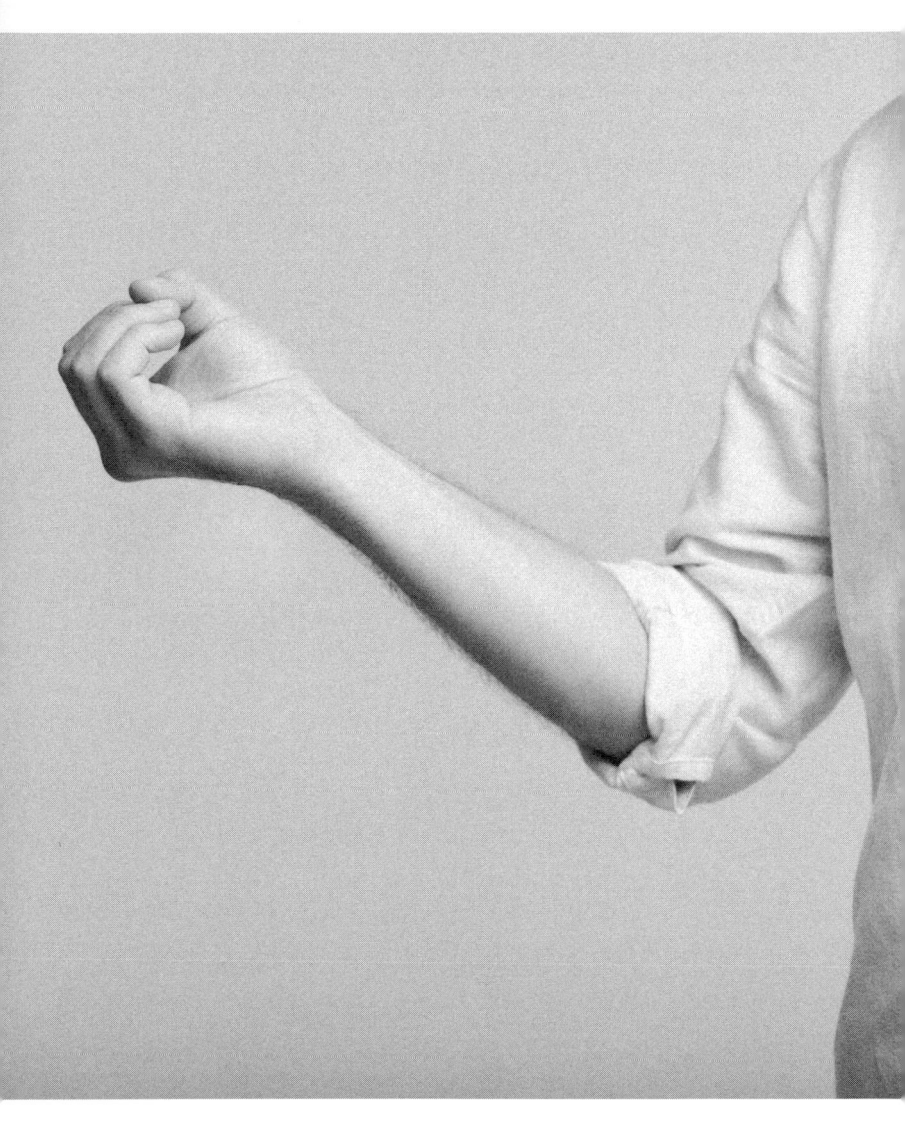

*"Go masturbate."*

# DICK HEAD

**Meaning:** You are a dick head.
**Used in:** United Kingdom

The unicorn is a rare mythical creature. This gesture, in which the forehead sports not a magical horn but an imaginary phallus, is an altogether more common and pedestrian event. To execute, simply bring the fingers and thumb together in a circle as if holding a phallus, and place hand near forehead. Often seen in pubs, at sporting matches, and in traffic altercations, it is used throughout the United Kingdom, where it serves, in the local parlance, to "take the piss" out of the subject.

*"You are a dick head."*

# ARM THRUST

**Meaning:** Prostitute
**Used in:** South America

It is in poor taste to comment on a woman's virtue, but if poor taste is your aim, this gesture will suit your purpose quite well. Hold the arm flat across the body with fingers extended and then quickly move the arm back and forth as though mimicking the thrusts of copulation. The resulting gesture suggests that the lady in question is a prostitute and that you yourself are a cad.

*"She's a prostitute."*

# THE CONCHA

**Meaning:** Your mother has dried-up lady parts
**Used in:** Chile, Argentina

In most of the world, this gesture simply means "hungry," but in Chile and Argentina, it means something quite different. This rather offensive gesture is short for *concha de tu madre* and refers to the "shell"—or love canal—of the subject's mother. The insult further implies that it is not a well-watered canal at all, but a dry riverbed.

*"Your mother has dried-up lady parts."*

107

# CORNA

**Meaning:** Your wife is unfaithful.
**Used in:** The Baltics, Brazil, Colombia, Italy, Portugal, Spain

Informing a friend that his wife has been unfaithful is an unhappy and delicate task. Fortunately, in many countries, it is simple to do: one simply gives him the Corna. A very old sign, the Corna dates back at least 2,500 years and represents a bull's horns (bulls were commonly castrated to make them calmer).

Be warned that while the gesture is used throughout the world, its meaning varies greatly from country to country. In many countries, it is simply an expression of good luck; in others, it demonstrates an affection for a certain sporting team or musical group. Should you be on the receiving end of the gesture, before you cast out your wife, remember that your pal may simply be saying she is a fan of American college football or heavy metal bands.

**NOTE:** In Saudi Arabia, Syria, and Lebanon, one makes a similar gesture with an identical meaning by fanning out the fingers and placing the hands by the ears to mimic a stag.

*"Your wife is unfaithful."*

# CUTIS

**Meaning:** Screw you and your whole family.
**Used in:** India, Pakistan

Should you find yourself in India or Pakistan, wishing to insult not just your host but your host's entire family, look no further than the Cutis gesture. Its origins are unknown, but its effect is swift and severe. Simply make a fist then flick the thumb off the front teeth while exclaiming *cutta!* ("Screw you!") In short order, you will find yourself ejected from the premises, your mission to offend thoroughly accomplished.

*"Screw you!"*

# FODEU

**Meaning:** We're screwed. Screw you.
**Used in:** Brazil, France, Italy, Spain, South America

*Fodeu*, a vulgar term meaning "screwed," can imply that things are all screwed up or that the subject should go screw himself. To make the gesture, pound the open palm of one hand on top of the fist of the other. The motion should mimic the thrusts of sexual intercourse.

*"We're screwed."*

# ONWARD AND UPWARD

With this chapter we arrive, quite literally, at the end, with a collection of gestures referencing the backside and its orifices. These gestures come from all over the world. For while every culture is different, almost all of them offer a gesture that suggests the subject ram something up his rectum. Some may call for a finger and some a forearm, and they vary with regard to circumference and force. But, ultimately, they all mean the same thing: "Up yours."

And this sentiment is also a very old one. Many of these gestures date back to ancient times, but the sentiment they convey is unchanged. It's a sentiment that's not even limited to our own species; some of these gestures are very similar to ones made by apes.

Although the message may be crude, it is nice to know that the same gesture would be understood by a chimpanzee, an ancient Roman, and a modern teenager. It is a happy reminder that while we may look different and talk differently, at bottom, we're all the same.

# BRAS D'HONNEUR

**Meaning:** Up yours.
**Used in:** Eastern Europe, Southern Europe, Mexico, Middle East

With a name that is French for "arm of honor," this gesture is known all over the world thanks to its on-field popularity with professional athletes. Signifying "Up yours," it is an outsize variation of the *doigt d'honneur* (or middle finger), whose grand scale makes it particularly well suited to arena sports. Be warned, however, that it remains illegal in some countries, such as Malta.

Despite its popularity among sportsmen, you need not be athletically inclined to use it yourself. Simply bend the arm at the elbow in an L-shape, using your other arm to grab on just below the bicep. If you wish to gild the lily, you may raise the middle finger of the bent arm.

*"Up yours."*

# FIST THRUST

**Meaning:** Up yours.
**Used in:** Lebanon, Pakistan, Syria

Yet another way of signaling "Up yours," this particular incarnation suggests a circumference and degree of force that most would find quite uncomfortable. A regional variation of the Bras d'Honneur (page 116), it is guaranteed to cause great offense in parts of the Middle East.

*"Up yours."*

119

# THUMBS-UP

**Meaning:** Up yours.
**Used in:** Greece, Latin America, Middle East, Russia, Sardinia, western Africa

Evolutionary biologists agree that the thumb originated millions of years ago. As for when the thumbs-up gesture originated, however, that remains unclear. Whatever its origins, its significance varies. Often, it just means approval. But in some countries, especially Latin American ones, it came to mean not "Sounds good" or "Could you give me a lift?" or "You should see this movie," but rather an invitation to insert the thumb intra-anally. Visitors to these regions should take care to keep their thumbs tucked well away unless offense is your intent. For extra insult, jerk upward.

**NOTE:** In Turkey, the gesture is often an invitation to homosexual relations.

*"Up yours."*

121

# V

**Meaning:** Up yours.
**Used in:** United Kingdom, Australia, New Zealand

Known as the "two-fingered salute" or the "forks," this gesture is particular to the United Kingdom and its former colonies. Scholars believe that the gesture may have originated during the Norman invasion. When English archers were captured, it's said the French would cut off their index and middle fingers. At the Battle of Agincourt, when the French were badly defeated, English archers taunted French soldiers by flashing their intact fingers, and thus, perhaps, the V gesture was born.

The V differs from the peace sign in that the palm faces in. The two should not be confused, as good vibes will not result.

*"Up yours."*

# FIG

**Meaning:** Up yours. Screw you. Would you like me to screw you?
**Used in:** Belgium, Denmark, France, Germany, Greece, Holland, India, Italy, Korea, Tunisia, Turkey

Known as the *fica* (or "fig") this gesture was common in ancient Rome, where it represented the reproductive sweetmeats, perhaps in the act of love. Over time it traveled to other countries; in some of which it was believed to have magical powers that could break spells and ward off evil.

The Fig remains a commonly used gesture throughout Europe and parts east, though its meaning varies from region to region. In some, it retains its original sexual connotation; in others, it is a good luck gesture meant to dispel bad fortune; and in still others, it is a profane insult. To execute, simply make a fist with the thumb protruding between the index and middle finger. Given the Fig's widely varying meanings, the savvy traveler will avoid playing "got your nose" with his host's children, lest an extremely awkward reaction result.

**NOTE:** In Japan, this is the sign for *sekkusu* (or "sex"). Its use in Japan is believed to date back to the Edo period (1603–1868), but it is rarely seen today.

*"Screw you."*

# OK

**Meaning:** Orifice
**Used in:** Brazil, Germany, Greece, Italy, Malta, Mexico, Middle East, Paraguay, Russia, Tunisia, Turkey

"OK" is a near-universal word. The OK gesture, however, does not translate as easily. For as the inexperienced traveler quickly learns, in many countries, it is not a gesture of approval, but a graphic representation of a delicate orifice. The orifice in question varies regionally—sometimes male and sometimes female, sometimes ventral and sometimes dorsal. The intent, however, is always crude and usually insulting.

*"Stick it in your orifice."*

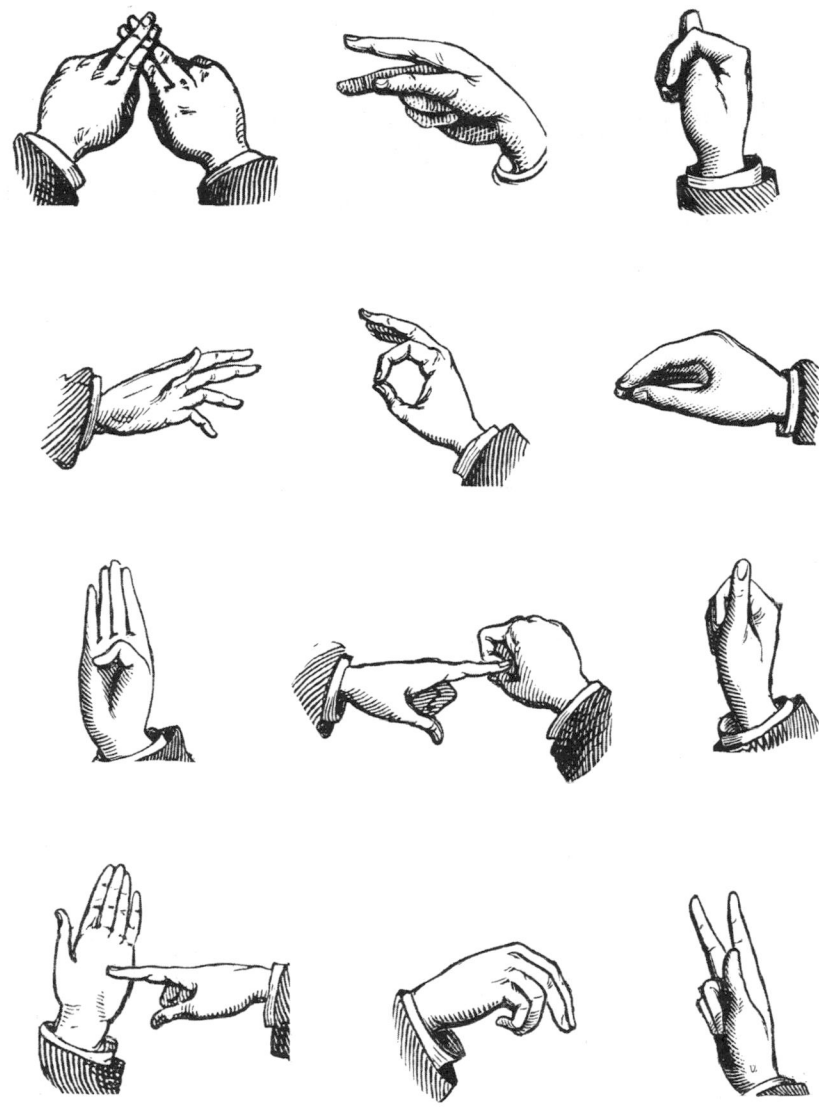

# RUDE HAND GESTURES OF THE WORLD